First Masterpiece of Chinese Painting

The Admonitions Scroll

FIRST MASTERPIECE OF CHINESE PAINTING

The Admonitions Scroll

Shane McCausland

George Braziller, Publishers
New York

'Fearful of the ascendancy of Empress Jia and her family, Zhang Hua
composed the "Admonitions of the Instructress to the Court Ladies" to reprove her.'

From the 'Biography of Zhang Hua', poet and statesman (AD 232–300), *History of the Jin Dynasty* (AD 646)

First published in the United States of America by George Braziller, Inc., in 2003.
Originally published in Great Britain by The British Museum Press in 2003.
The Trustees of The British Museum gratefully acknowledge the generous support
of the E. Rhodes and Leona B. Carpenter Foundation
© 2003 The Trustees of The British Museum

For information, please address the publisher:
George Braziller, Inc.
171 Madison Avenue
New York, NY 10016

Library of Congress Cataloguing-in-Publication Data:
McCausland, Shane, 1968–
First masterpiece of Chinese painting : the Admonitions scroll /
by Shane McCausland.
p. cm.
Includes bibliographical references and index.
ISBN 0-8076-1517-X (hb)
1. Gu, Kaizhi, 344–405. Admonitions of the instructress to the court ladies.
2. Gu, Kaizhi, 344–405.—Criticism and interpretation.
3. Zhang, Hua, 232–300. Nè shi zhen—Illustrations.
4. Scrolls, Chinese—Three kingdoms—Sui dynasty, 220–618.
I. Gu, Kaizhi, 344–405. II. Title.
ND2070.G8A636 2003
759.951—dc22   2003052387

Frontispiece: Blue brocade outer-wrapper for the Qianlong mounting of the *Admonitions* scroll
of *c.* 1746. The wrapper originally bore a title-slip in the calligraphy of the Qianlong emperor
(r. 1736–95) identifying the *Admonitions* as the work of Gu Kaizhi (*c.* 344–*c.* 406).

Designed and typeset in Walbaum by Andrew Shoolbred Ltd
Printed in Spain by Grafos SA
First edition

Contents

Preface

In the four hundred years between the collapse of the Han empire (206 BC–AD 220) in the third century and the reunification of the country under the Tang dynasty (618–906) in the seventh century, an era known as the Period of Disunion, China experienced a dramatic change in the development of art and art theories. With the decline of Confucianism, the mystic philosophies of native Daoism and imported Buddhism captured the imagination of Chinese scholars and artists who, disillusioned with life at the court, chose to turn away from political engagement and devote themselves to the appreciation of nature and the pursuit of artistic expression. Under the Eastern Jin (317–420), one of the six Southern dynasties that ruled southern China in this period of political fragmentation, lived one of China's greatest artistic geniuses, the painter Gu Kaizhi (c. 344–c. 406), who is celebrated as the founding father of classical Chinese figure painting.

Admonitions of the Instructress to the Court Ladies (Nüshi zhen tu), a handscroll traditionally attributed to Gu Kaizhi, now in the British Museum, can today be identified through comparative archaeological evidence as a late sixth-century Southern court copy of the original. Recorded in Mi Fu's (1052–1107) *History of Painting (Huashi)* and the Northern Song (960–1127) *Catalogue of the Imperial Painting Collection During the Xuanhe Era (Xuanhe huapu)* of 1120 as an original work by Gu, and bearing impressions of an authenticated imperial palace seal – 'Ruisi dongge' (Palace of Sagacious Contemplation, East Wing), dated between 1075 and 1078 – the scroll displays the distinctively taut and masterful brush style that was instantly recognizable in later times as the famous 'gossamer brush line' historically associated with the legendary ancient master by Chinese connoisseurs. As such, it was treasured by the eighteenth-century Qing emperor Qianlong (r. 1736–95) as the earliest and most important masterwork in his vast palace collection of classical Chinese paintings.

Traditional Chinese connoisseurship stressed the concept of the 'trace of the brush' (*biji*), which held that both calligraphy and painting represented the physical presence of their maker. The 'trace' of a great artist – for example, Gu's 'gossamer brush line' – was thought to embody material proof of his genius, or even immortality. The material 'trace' of Gu Kaizhi was first preserved in tracing copies of his painting. Through the 'spiritual response' (*shenhui*) of the copyist and that of the viewer the original act of the artist was thus recreated. This practice of copying helps to explain the remarkable continuity of Chinese art and culture over the centuries, in which the artistic process of replication parallels the anthropological (and biological) concept of genealogy. The styles of the canonical masters, as transmitted through tracing copies and replicas, may be thought of as a kind of DNA imprint from which all subsequent idioms emerge. By achieving the 'spiritual likeness' (*shensi*) of an ancient master, a later master brings that artist back to life.

At the June 2001 international colloquy on the scroll, jointly organized by the British Museum and the Percival David Foundation of Chinese Art, some twenty scholars presented papers examining the many vexing problems surrounding the *Admonitions of the Instructress to the Court Ladies*: its relation to the fourth-century painter Gu Kaizhi, the date of its creation, the literary and seal evidence relating to the scroll, and the 'cultural biography' of the work from the Song period (960–1276) onward. The concept of the biography of an object owes much, in its materialist approach, to the discipline of anthropology. Rather than asking when, where, and by whom the object was made, it is concerned with the processes of 'reception', or telling the story of how an object was viewed in a later socio-historical context.

In the present publication Shane McCausland shows how an attentive and well-informed examination of the *Admonitions* scroll can provide information about

Gu Kaizhi and the history of Chinese painting. He explains how through Gu's genius, as recaptured in the scroll by the sixth-century copyist, ancient Chinese painting achieved what the Grand Guardian Xie An (320–85) described as a miraculous breakthrough to 'something that had never been seen before', and how, through the visual evidence of the scroll, later Chinese painters pursued their own course of creativity in Chinese art history. By taking us step by step through the visual (i.e. material and physical) evidence of text and image, McCausland helps us to find a way through the complexities posed by art history and historiography in order to arrive at a 'spiritual response' to the painting. While it may not convince every reader of the very presence of Gu Kaizhi in the *Admonitions* scroll, this publication will without question contribute to a wider and deeper appreciation of one of the great treasures of ancient Chinese art.

Wen C. Fong
Princeton University and
The Metropolitan Museum of Art,
Emeritus

Acknowledgements

Writing this book would not have been possible without the contributions to research on the *Admonitions* scroll and Gu Kaizhi of the scholars who participated in the June 2001 colloquium at the British Museum, and I should like to acknowledge that body of work with thanks. I also reiterate here my thanks to the sponsors of that event, the Chiang Ching-kuo Foundation for International Scholarly Exchange, the British Academy, and the School of Oriental and African Studies and the Percival David Foundation of Chinese Art in the University of London. Additionally, this publication would not have appeared without the assistance and support of members of the curatorial staff in the Department of Asia (formerly the Department of Oriental Antiquities) at the British Museum, including Jane Portal and Carol Michaelson, Assistant Keepers, and Robert Knox, Keeper. Fine new photography of the *Admonitions* scroll was provided by the Museum's Department of Photography and Imaging. Additional photography was provided by Glenn Ratcliffe. Sophie Sorrendegui and the Museum Assistants have also helped in numerous ways with production.

The publication of this volume is made possible by a generous subvention from the E. Rhodes and Leona B. Carpenter Foundation via the American Friends of the British Museum. John and Julia Curtis and Giuseppe Eskenazi kindly helped at different stages. The imaginative design of the book was created by Andrew Shoolbred. The text was copy-edited with care by Coralie Hood. At British Museum Press, the credit goes to Bill Jones, Sarah Levesley and the excellent production team, to Alasdair Macleod and to Nina Shandloff, whose editorial skills have guided the book from conception to publication. Judy Inn, Maggie Chui Ki Wan and Zhang Yi variously assisted with production in many important ways.

For their intellectual community, I am indebted to colleagues in the Department of Art and Archaeology and elsewhere at SOAS, and in the Sainsbury Institute for the Study of Japanese Arts and Cultures, including John Carpenter, Nicole Rousmaniere and Timon Screech. I owe a debt of thanks to John Carpenter, Wen Fong, Robert Knox and Stacey Pierson, and especially to Sarah Wong, for their supportive contributions to the publication of this book. It is dedicated to Sarah.

Shane McCausland
Bloomsbury
Summer 2003

1 | Why Gu Kaizhi?

This book is about a painting entitled the *Admonitions of the Instructress to the Court Ladies* attributed to the great early master of the Chinese figural tradition, Gu Kaizhi (*c.* 344–*c.* 406). A narrative-type painting, the *Admonitions* illustrates episodes of an eighty-line poem about Confucian virtue-ethics, a text composed in AD 292 by the savant and courtier Zhang Hua (232–300) to admonish Empress Jia (256–300), ruthless wife of the young emperor of the Western Jin dynasty (265–316), Huidi (r. 290–306). According to the dynastic history of this period, *History of the Jin*, Zhang Hua, a loyal minister, saw how Empress Jia and her clan were usurping the authority of the deluded emperor and jeopardizing the stability of the dynasty, already under threat from a civil war among the Jin princes. Fearful of the consequences of Empress Jia's actions, Zhang Hua wrote his reproving poem-memorial in order to correct her behaviour. Both Empress Jia and Zhang Hua met their deaths following a coup led by one of the imperial princes in 300. Not long after, Zhang Hua's 'Admonitions' poem was illustrated in the form of a picture-scroll for the instruction of empresses, consorts and imperial concubines in their proper role and conduct.

A scroll of this title is first mentioned in writing at the beginning of the twelfth century when, on account of its consummate 'archaic, hairline' ink-outline and simple colour wash, it was described as the masterpiece of Gu Kaizhi, who lived about a century after Zhang Hua and Empress Jia in the Eastern Jin dynasty (317–420). The use of this fine, swirling outline style in the incisive portrayals of emperors and court ladies, often in dramatic encounters, exemplifies Gu Kaizhi's renowned ability to 'capture the spirit' of his subjects. However, although the painting is richly informed by personal experience of medieval court life, such as Gu Kaizhi had, the somewhat more sophisticated modelling of the figures and the use of certain pictorial designs place the work in the late fifth or sixth century AD. It was painted by an unknown artist,

1 ■ Emperor from the 'rejection' scene, the *Admonitions* scroll.

故曰翼翼矜矜福所以興靜恭自思榮顯所期

perhaps a courtier-painter like Gu Kaizhi, who may have been copying an original by Gu Kaizhi or else working in the tradition of the earlier master, while incorporating contemporary techniques and devices. The inscriptions of Zhang Hua's 'Admonitions' that accompany each illustration were executed at the same time as the paintings, probably by a court calligrapher or scribe. The late Six Dynasties (220–589) style of the calligraphy – examined in chapter 3 – strongly suggests the *Admonitions* originated at one of the southern courts of China in this period. By far the earliest scroll-painting in the Chinese painting tradition, the *Admonitions* seems to be the only surviving masterpiece of Six Dynasties painting.

In addition to being recorded in around 1100, the *Admonitions* has a well-documented provenance through imperial, official and private collections since that time. Illustrating a special feature of the Chinese handscroll format, the painting is accompanied by silk mounting panels bearing impressions of seals of collectors and connoisseurs through whose hands the artwork passed, as well as a number of their own paintings and inscriptions on attached lengths of silk and paper, which were incorporated into the handscroll mounting at various dates in transmission. 'The *Admonitions* scroll' – by which we mean this composite object – is today preserved in the British Museum in London, which bought it for the sum of £25 in 1903 from an Indian Army cavalry officer who had acquired it in Peking in 1900 after the Boxer Rebellion (1899–1900). Beautiful, ancient, powerful, exemplary, this important arte-fact tells a unique story of the history of art in China.

While it is agreed to be, in short, one of the great relics of early Chinese art, gaining a precise understanding of such issues as its date, authorship, rhetoric and provenance has proved less straightforward. The first chapter of this book asks 'Why Gu Kaizhi?': why is the painting ascribed to the legendary artist Gu Kaizhi, the father of China's classical tradition? We now know it is not by him (because of the pictorial innovations that post-date his period of activity), but it is important to understand how the painting relates to him, and why the attribution stands. The second chapter inves-tigates the *Admonitions* painting itself and what it tells us about the beginning of the art of painting in China. It considers the textual source for the painting, the individual scenes of admonitions, the insightful portraits of rulers and their beautiful consorts, and the lyrical linear style. It focuses on the *Admonitions* scroll in London, which com-prises the paintings and calligraphic inscriptions of the last nine scenes. Originally twelve scenes, the first three and the text of the fourth were lost possibly as early as the eleventh century. The missing scenes are examined with the help of a twelfth-century copy of the scroll in the Palace Museum, Beijing. The third chapter examines the inscriptions of the 'Admonitions' text on the painting, the importance of which guaranteed the scroll's survival in at least one phase of its transmission. The fourth chapter traces the artwork's life-history as it passed through the hands of collectors and connoisseurs over many dynasties since its probable creation in fifth- or sixth-century China. It explores the written notes, seals and paintings that they added to the scroll and asks how, in time, the *Admonitions* scroll has come to be so significant for the understanding of Chinese art history. The epilogue considers the position of Gu Kaizhi and the *Admonitions* in the modern world.

Gu Kaizhi and the classical tradition of Chinese painting

Gu Kaizhi stands for the beginning of classical Chinese painting. He lived at a transitional moment of Chinese history between the great Han (206 BC–AD 220) and Tang (618–907) empires, in a period of rapid cultural and political change known as the Six Dynasties or Period of Disunion. Gu himself lived under one of the era's short-lived southern dynasties, the Eastern Jin (317–420), a founding, classical era in both painting and calligraphy. Even when he was still a young man, Gu Kaizhi's painting was described by one of the literary giants of his day, the Grand Guardian Xie An (320–85), as marking a new beginning. 'Your painting', Xie told him, 'is like nothing that has ever been seen before!' Like many of his contemporaries, Gu Kaizhi took to the arts to seek refuge from the uncertainties of the day, and was also valued for his rapier wit and foolishness. Gu Kaizhi once lampooned his own conventional show of grief with the remark that upon hearing news of his patron's death, a wind howled through his nose and his eyes cried rivers. It is not surprising that in history he should have become known as the archetypal flamboyant genius – a figure conjured out of stories about him and paintings believed to be by his hand.

It is also insightful that creativity in China should be identified not with pictorial techniques of illusion, but with an artist's finding a lyrical, personal voice. Up to this date, most pictures had been images incised into stone or painted in lacquer; painters and even calligraphers were generally considered artisans. Gu Kaizhi lived at

2 ▪ Mi Fu (*c.* 1052–1107).
'Self-Portrait'. Rubbing from
an engraving at Fubo Hill,
Guilin, Guangxi Province.

a time when the writing/painting brush and the media of paper and silk had just come into common usage (something that would last until the early twentieth century). In the hands of calligraphers and painters among the southern gentry, these media opened up a new expressive world. Historically, the core of Gu Kaizhi's creativity was seen to be the way his use of these tools broke the classical mould of image-making, in that he used them to inscribe his education and wit – his self – into what now became the art of painting.

We duly find Gu Kaizhi recorded in first histories of painting, written by critics from the later Six Dynasties period on. They tell of a foursome of early figure-painting masters between the fourth and eighth centuries: 'Gu, Lu, Zhang and Wu', referring to Gu Kaizhi, together with Lu Tanwei (act. *c.* 465–72), Zhang Sengyou of the Liang dynasty (502–57), and the 'Painting Sage' Wu Daozi (eighth century) of the Tang dynasty (618–907). The ninth-century painter and critic Zhang Yanyuan wrote: 'The spiritual expressiveness of Gu and Lu is boundless, because their drawings are always complete and finely finished, while the wonders of Zhang and Wu lie in their ability to capture images with only one or two abbreviated brushstrokes …' This art historian was already dividing the history of painting into stages, seeing the earlier two masters as having worked in a 'complete and finely finished' style, and the later two as using 'abbreviated brushstrokes'. Although no paintings by any of these four masters are extant, in what follows we will try to use the *Admonitions* attributed to Gu Kaizhi and other early paintings that have survived to understand the visual changes Zhang Yanyuan sought to explain.

Since at least the eleventh century Gu Kaizhi's name has been linked with this painting entitled the *Admonitions of the Instructress to the Court Ladies (Nüshi zhen tu)*. The association was made in a book called the *History of Painting (Hua shi)* of 1103 by Mi Fu (1052–1107), the artist, collector and notorious doyen of the late Northern Song (960–1127) art world. Although Mi Fu's motives in almost all his endeavours have long been questioned, to him, the archaic 'gossamer' outline style and the subject of the *Admonitions* could only have signalled the hand of Gu Kaizhi. It was a seductive link, and one that the passage of time and the ever-greater distance from Gu Kaizhi have merely intensified. Mi Fu moved in the circle of leading literati artists including the scholar-painter Li Gonglin (*c.* 1041–1106), the foremost later follower of Gu Kaizhi's painting, as well as the court, where many old master works – including the

Admonitions – were kept. Mi would have known as much about Gu Kaizhi as anyone could at that time, and was a key promoter of his reputation. In fact, Mi Fu so admired Gu Kaizhi's 'lofty antiquity' that, for his self-portrait, preserved in the worn engraving in figure 2, he even modelled himself on one of the figures of an emperor in the *Admonitions* scroll, thus doubly connecting his own image with Gu Kaizhi's for posterity. Later studies of the *Admonitions* have indeed proceeded from Mi Fu's attribution of it to Gu Kaizhi. In our time, we may also use comparative archaeological evidence to explore how this painting relates to innovations in Six Dynasties painting, and in that light, how its style relates to the revolutionary talent of Gu Kaizhi discussed by the early critics.

Gu Kaizhi continues to be a legend in China today, where he remains a founding figure in the history of painting. Painters still begin to learn the fundamental outline technique executed with the traditional media of brush and ink on silk or paper by copying 'Gu Kaizhi'. Perhaps the sense of continuity that this gives to our notion of Chinese culture is deceptive, especially in light of the complex picture of political and social upheaval that is historical China. Indeed, what seems to have guaranteed the longevity of the name of Gu Kaizhi is controversy, and we should not assume his reputation has gone unchanged, or unchallenged throughout history. In fact, we might say that it is only through conversations in words and images about pivotal figures like Gu Kaizhi that definitions of big issues such as art and culture may be approached.

The celebration of Gu Kaizhi's talents in Chinese educational book illustration in the 1990s is a case in point, for it undoubtedly draws upon a popular modern picture-book tradition in China. At the same time, reviving memories of the heroes of ancient culture also compensated for the irretrievable loss of the past in cities such as Shanghai and Beijing, where the traditional domestic architecture of the old districts

3 ■ Wu Sheng (b. 1943, Suzhou). *Gu Kaizhi Transmits the Spirit by Dotting the Eye*, dated 1992. Picture-book illustration for 'Gu Kaizhi, the earliest great painter', pp. 21–2 in *The Charisma of Art (Yishu de fengcai)*, vol. 7 of the *Arts* section of the series, *Highlights of Stories from Traditional Chinese Culture (Zhongguo chuantong wenhua, gushi huicui)* (Hangzhou, 1994).

had suddenly disappeared to make way for high-rise blocks, malls and business parks. In one 1994 picture-book illustration (fig. 3), Gu Kaizhi is shown about to 'transmit the spirit' to his first great painting, a portrait of the Buddhist layman Vimalakirti produced in the early 360s for the newly-built Tile Coffin Temple (Waguansi) in the southern city of Nanjing, capital of the Eastern Jin dynasty in which Gu lived.

At this time, as during much of the Six Dynasties period, both Buddhism and the arts flourished, and hundreds of temples were being built, renovated or expanded all over China, although none survives today. During construction, the monks of the Tile Coffin Temple appealed to patrons for funds to cover the costs. The offer of 'a million cash' by the unknown painter Gu Kaizhi was at first seen as laughable. When asked how he would pay, he demanded a blank wall within the temple to work on. Shutting himself away for a month, Gu Kaizhi completed a mural of the great Indian sage Vimalakirti, a most sympathetic figure to Chinese converts to Buddhism, for his having reconciled being a wealthy man with being a devout Buddhist.

After a month, Gu Kaizhi's mural was finished, and he instructed the Tile Coffin Temple monks to charge viewers a hundred thousand cash on the first day, ten thousand on the second, and thereafter whatever they could contribute. When the doors were opened, 'radiance filled the entire temple' and 'donors blocked the hallways': the temple soon collected the pledged 'million cash', but Gu Kaizhi also made his reputation. In the 1994 book illustration Gu is seen accompanied by an old monk of the temple, preparing to perform the eye-dotting ceremony. To 'dot the eye' of a deity's statue or portrait was the usual way that its spirit was summoned into it, bringing it to life. Another of the stories about Gu Kaizhi has it that he often left the eyes of his figures undotted for years, while he decided how he would animate a figure. Gu wrote that 'transmitting the spirit in a portrait lies in the eye'. What is so remarkable about the figures in the *Admonitions* scroll is that the eye contact between them or the direction of their gazes is what actually makes the expression in their looks, body language, posture and bearing complete. The atmospheric clouds of cosmic mist and ether in the 1992 illustration describe the indescribable – the spirit of Vimalakirti being summoned – but conveniently also mean that the portrait cannot be seen. However, the early sources on painting aver that after Gu Kaizhi, all pictures of Vimalakirti were modelled after his. Vimalakirti was invariably depicted in later times displaying his mastery of abstruse Buddhist doctrine, as in the Tang dynasty cave

4 ■ 'Vimalakirti'. Mural in Cave 103, Dunhuang, Gansu Province. Tang dynasty, mid-8th century.

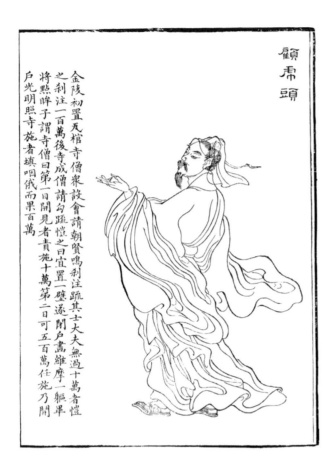

顧愷頭

金陵初置瓦棺寺僧眾設會請朝賢鳴剎
之剎注一百萬後寺成僧請勾踈愷之曰宜置一壁遂
將點眸子謂寺僧第一日開見者責施十萬第二日可
戶光明照寺施者填咽俄而果百萬
五百萬任施乃開

5 ■ Shangguan Zhou (1665–1749). 'Gu Kaizhi', from *Painting Manual of the Hall of Old-age Smiles*. Qing dynasty, 18th-century edition. School of Oriental and African Studies Library, University of London.

mural in figure 4, which is presumably a version after Gu Kaizhi's original.

The image of a public-spirited Gu Kaizhi about to dot the eye of his *Vimalakirti* at the Tile Coffin Temple is a popular modern one that took shape over the course of the Manchu dynasty in China, the Qing (1644–1911). The powerful but sanctimonious Qianlong emperor (r. 1736–95) acquired the *Admonitions* scroll – then believed to be Gu Kaizhi's masterpiece – in the mid-1740s. Although the emperor enshrined the painting at the pinnacle of Chinese painting history, an issue to which we return below, he cared less about the artist, whose reputation for practical jokes and ribaldry ran counter to the moral and political lessons he was seen to be learning from the scroll. At about the same date, the painter and book illustrator Shangguan Zhou (1665–1749) rescued and fortified the popular conception of Gu Kaizhi as an unconventional genius in his woodblock-printed copybook, *Painting Manual of the Hall of Old-age Smiles* (fig. 5), an anthology of portraits and biographies published in the early 1740s. Employing Gu Kaizhi's trademark thin tensile lines to render the billowing drapery, Shangguan Zhou presents the artist as a distinguished figure – too distinguished for an unknown painter in his twenties! – who gestures grandly towards his *Vimalakirti* with an outstretched arm. Gu Kaizhi's expansive manner conjures up the scene about him: a throng of donors filling the hall and the clamour of their response to his mural. Here was Gu Kaizhi as a celebrity artist, and subject of the first 'blockbuster' exhibition.

'Describing spirit through form'

In Chinese art history, Gu Kaizhi is closely associated with the painterly concept of 'transmitting the spirit' to figures. He is also said to have excelled in having 'described

spirit through form' in his subjects. His figure of Vimalakirti was not just lifelike or seemingly real; more importantly, it had 'breath resonance' with the subject. After the eye was dotted, the portrait became a body for the real presence of the figure. In one of the well-known anecdotes told about Gu Kaizhi, he employed his extraordinary skill at creating this resonance to get his neighbour, a young woman, to return his feelings for her. He succeeded by painting a close likeness of her on his wall and pricking the figure through the heart with a pin. The woman complained to him of heartache, whereupon he removed the pin and 'the matter was resolved'. The charismatic figures of empresses and emperors in the *Admonitions* scroll are among the best surviving indications of how this heightened interest in the human mind and spirit in the Six

6 ■ *Tales from History and Legends.* Detail of a lintel tile; ink and colour on whitened ground, 73.3 × 240.7 cm. Western Han dynasty, late 1st century BC. Museum of Fine Arts, Boston (Denman Waldo Ross collection 25.10–13 and Gift of C.T. Loo 25.190).

Dynasties period manifested itself in the portrayal of the human body in figure paint-ing. This interest is confirmed in archaeologically recovered pictures such as the tomb mural in Boston (fig. 6).

From the late Six Dynasties and into the Tang period, critics immortalized Gu Kaizhi for this spiritual dimension in his work. It was not long after Gu Kaizhi's life-time that some of the founding principles of Chinese painting were written down in the form of the critic and painter Xie He's Six Laws. The first of these is, literally, 'breath resonance – life motion' (*qiyun shengdong*), which holds that when the spirit of the figure painted resonates with its subject, the figure will have the vital presence of the living subject. The insights into the characters of the emperors and ladies in the *Admonitions* painting as revealed through the portraits fulfil this ideal like no other early painting. A portrait painter himself, Xie He considered Gu Kaizhi to be highly overrated, a verdict that has produced indignant protest and compensatory praise for Gu from critics ever since. The later sixth-century critic Yao Zui first praised Gu Kaizhi –

> When it comes to praising one such as Gu Kaizhi, one can only say that he com-mands the highest place in the records of the past and stands lofty and alone. In all time he had no equal. He has a sort of supernatural brilliance, which ordi-nary intelligence could never hope to realise … No one has ever been seen who could meet him on equal terms.

– before rounding on Xie He:

> That Xie He records of him 'his fame exceeded the reality' is quite depressing enough, but that he should have placed Gu in one of the low classes [of paint-ing] is something which I can bear with even less equanimity.

The early eighth-century critic Zhang Huaiguan wrote:

> Because Master Gu imagined his painting in such a fine and subtle way, the depths of his spiritual expression are unfathomable. Though he left his traces in brush and ink, his spirit flies high above the cloudy firmament, so it cannot be sought merely in his painting. In creating beautiful images, Zhang Sengyou captures the flesh, Lu Tanwei the bone, but only Gu Kaizhi the spirit. It is in the incomparable marvels of his spiritual expressiveness that Gu's works excel.

Beyond the idea that his figures had a strong 'bone' or skeletal structure, it is not clear what Lu Tanwei's painting looked like – although we may note that Lu Tanwei was highly rated by Xie He, and the principle that 'bone structure – [this lies in] use of the brush' was the second of the Six Laws. The 'flesh'-like quality of the figures of Zhang Sengyou, the eminent court painter under the southern Liang dynasty, must have been related to the Western *chiaroscuro* technique imported from the West in his time. Created by painting shaded bands of colour, this technique described surfaces with an accuracy that had never been seen before. By comparison with these two, Gu Kaizhi's painting was still 'complete and finely detailed' and yet captured the 'spirit' – the personality and character conveyed through an individual's mien, bearing and body language.

The valuing of presentation (of the self) over representation (of the world) in a work of art marks a fundamental difference from the way the ancient Greeks thought about painting and sculpture – and, after them, artists in the European tradition, until recently. In the western world, a work of art was an imitation, something that re-presented a subject through visual techniques of illusion and deception, in which all traces of the process of manufacture, such as brush strokes, were covered up. In the case of Gu Kaizhi, the network of silk hairline brush strokes that describe his figures is patently revealed as a technical scheme, a manner of controlling the brush (see fig. 1). In fact, Gu Kaizhi's painting was compared by critics such as Zhang Huaiguan to the pioneering brush calligraphy of the Han dynasty (206 BC–AD 220). In dynastic China, the traces of a great individual's writing brush were deeply venerated as the embodi-ment of their creator. The analogy of calligraphy illustrates how complex and subtle, and indeed how human Gu Kaizhi's hairline brushwork was understood to be. These delicate brush lines in the *Admonitions* represent the figures, their attitudes, expres-sions and bearing, and convey the artist's psychological insights into their characters. At the same time, their independent qualities – including their archaic hairline thin-ness and swirling rhythms – were seen as calligraphic signs that did not stand in for but actually embodied the artist, Gu Kaizhi.

The ninth-century critic and painter Zhang Yanyuan described Gu Kaizhi's drawing style as

> tight and sinewy, smooth and continuous; it circles around and disappears [into the painted image]. Its manner is as untrammelled and easy as a wafting breeze

or quick lightning, always with an idea guiding his brush so that the idea remains even after his brush ends. This is why his paintings are full of a spiritual air.

In a sense, the critics approved more of painting about 'spirit' – that which unites humanity across time – and less about advances in techniques of representation, which were achievements of the moment. As this ideal became more entrenched in art history, Gu Kaizhi's position as the ancestor of painting was affirmed and reaffirmed.

The making of the *Admonitions* scroll

There is the important art-historical question of when the original illustration of the *Admonitions* was painted, but there are also the related historical questions, 'how?' and 'why?'. Its volatile subject matter suggests it was commissioned as a warning to the consorts at one of the courts of medieval China, either in Gu Kaizhi's lifetime or later, because it illustrates a text composed for this purpose in the year 292 by the savant and poet Zhang Hua. Appalled by the increasingly violent and immoral behaviour of the Empress Jia, wife of the young emperor Huidi, Zhang Hua saw it as his duty, as a senior minister, to caution her. Although this eighty-line poem, entitled 'Admonitions of the Instructress to the Court Ladies' ('Nüshi zhen'), had little effect on her – Empress Jia continued to murder and plot against rivals and opponents until brought down in a coup in 300 – Zhang Hua's loyal remonstrating essay set an example of upright behaviour, both for ladies of the harem and male courtiers.

Assuming the first illustration was made about a century after the Zhang Hua poem, in Gu Kaizhi's lifetime, it was likely to have been a response to similar acts of outrageous behaviour by an empress or consort, such as murder or arrogating power to herself. That well-known admonitory images were quite standardized across China by the Six Dynasties became clear in 1986. This was when a lacquer screen depicting one of the scenes in the *Admonitions* (Lady Ban) was unearthed in the tomb of a Northern Wei (386–534) courtier called Sima Jinlong (d. 474), who was interred with his wife in 484 (fig. 7). The screen buried with them had been painted by artisans working in lacquer, a quite different context from the court-sponsored project that produced the *Admonitions* scroll, although it surely served a similar moral purpose.

7 ■ Stories of exemplary conduct: *(top to bottom)* stories of sage-king Shun; three meritorious mothers of Zhou; Chun Jiang, teacher of the State of Lu, and her daughter; Lady Ban declines to ride in the emperor's palanquin. Panel of a lacquer-painted wooden screen from the tomb of Sima Jinlong and his wife, approximately 80 × 20 cm. Datong, Shanxi Province. Northern Wei dynasty, before AD 484.

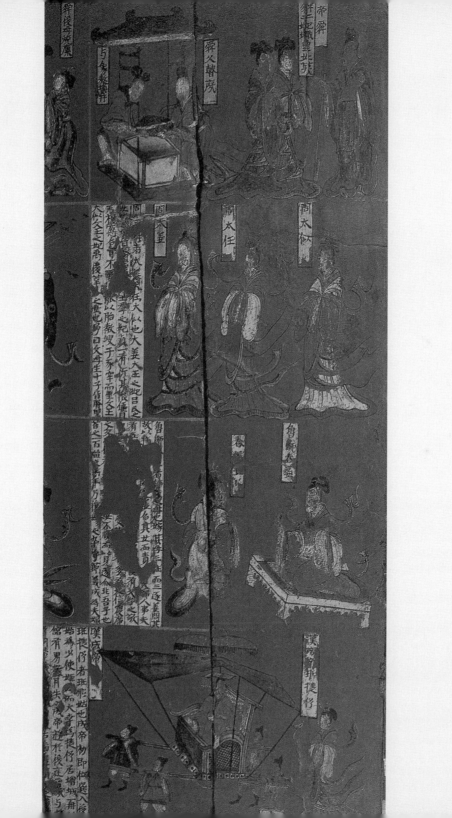

While plotting and double-dealing were common enough tactics in the shifting alliances among rival princes and warlords of this period, it was supposedly most irregular for the refined ladies of the imperial harem to resort to these means to further their own political careers. Beauty, at this time, was indeed seen as virtue. However, such events did occur at the Eastern Jin court with which Gu Kaizhi was connected, and it is in response to one of these that he could have been engaged to illustrate the 'Admonitions' text as a lesson to the ladies of the harem.

According to the *History of the Jin*, one of the most shocking examples took place in 396, after the emperor Xiaowudi (r. 372–96) teased his favourite, Lady Zhang, with the words: 'Now that you have reached thirty, I should exchange you for someone younger!' His suggestion that the full bloom of her beauty was now over put her in a jealous rage; she murdered the emperor the same evening. She was never brought to justice, but the court was scandalized by the violence of her revenge. Commissioning so direct a response as the 'Admonitions' in the form of a scroll-painting was the court's attempt to re-educate women on their proper roles and aspirations within the dynastic system. The painting, and the copies of it that were disseminated thereafter, served as a formidable tool of instruction then and throughout the later dynastic period.

Gu Kaizhi himself was well placed to have received this serious commission. Until he finally received an official post at court shortly before his death in about 406, he had the nominal protection and patronage of a succession of the Eastern Jin's ruling politician generals, whom he served as a painter and advisor. Gu Kaizhi's sense of humour was perhaps his most effective weapon in this role, for although he was a highly educated member of the elite, his lower rank left him vulnerable to their whims. On one occasion, he entrusted a chest of his most treasured paintings to Huan Xuan (369–404), a later patron and the son of one his earlier patrons, Huan Wen (312–73), with whom Gu is said to have burned the midnight oil discussing calligraphy. When Gu Kaizhi discovered that Huan Xuan had stolen some of the paintings by unscrewing the back of the chest but leaving his seal unbroken, he quipped, 'These paintings were supernatural marvels, so they must have flown off like people who have become transformed into immortals!' People used to say of Gu Kaizhi that he had 'three perfections – he was a perfect painter, a perfect wit, and a perfect fool'.

Gu Kaizhi's wit and foolishness no doubt helped to extricate him from such awkward situations, as well as to advance his career in flamboyant Eastern Jin society.

Like the Huans, Gu Kaizhi's other major patron, Yin Zhongkan, was enamoured of the arts and literature, and collected art avidly. A man of poor eyesight, Yin Zhongkan at first refused Gu's offer of a portrait, but relented when the winsome Gu declared the eyes would appear like 'moons obscured by light clouds'. The portrait of another of Gu's subjects, a learned scholar called Pei Kai, became celebrated when Gu added three fictitious hairs to Pei Kai's cheek which he said 'made the wise man look wise'. Doubtless Gu Kaizhi would have had the talent and imagination to execute such a delicate commission as the *Admonitions*.

Oeuvre

The titles of paintings by Gu Kaizhi in the early literature on painting – books like Zhang Yanyuan's *Record of Famous Painters of Successive Dynasties* of 847 – tell us that he painted portraits of his patrons and earlier men he admired, as well as Buddhist, Daoist and Confucian figure and narrative subjects, landscapes, and animals such as horses. Apart from the *Admonitions* scroll, which may be just a small step away from the historical Gu Kaizhi, these works are known only through copies, or copies of copies, or via tomb murals. Gu's own murals of Buddhist and Daoist figures in temples have long since disappeared – even Zhang Yanyuan in the ninth century hardly knew them. Gu Kaizhi's *Vimalakirti* at the Tile Coffin Temple can only be imagined from the iconographic image seen in later versions of the subject, for instance (fig. 4). Gu's portraits of his contemporaries and historical figures he admired, which are mentioned in anecdotes about his life, are unknown but for one important re-creation in archaic style done in the context of the late thirteenth-century renaissance of the arts. This painting, *Mind Landscape of Xie Youyu* by Zhao Mengfu (1254–1322) (see fig. 58 on page 102), as well as other early modern artists' visual 'dialogues' with Gu Kaizhi are taken up in chapter 3.

There are two categories of scroll-paintings ascribed to Gu Kaizhi that have come down to our time. The first comprises illustrations of texts about Confucian virtue-ethics for women. It includes two *Admonitions* paintings, the one in London, and a monochrome copy believed to be a twelfth-century copy in the Palace Museum, Beijing (fig. 8), and another Song-dynasty copy of an earlier painting in the same museum, entitled *Benevolent and Wise Women* (fig. 9). The portraits in *Benevolent and*

8 ■ Southern Song court artists (painter and scribe), later 12th century. *Admonitions of the Instructress to the Court Ladies.* Traditionally attributed to Li Gonglin (*c.* 1049–1106). Handscroll; ink on paper, 27.9 × 600.5 cm. Palace Museum, Beijing.

Wise Women are conceived and rendered like the *Admonitions* figures: we see small scenes, usually without setting, featuring women in striking postures with hour-glass figures, elaborate coiffures, and many-layered dresses with thick folds and ribbons. Stylistically, the *Benevolent and Wise Women* painting is akin to the Beijing *Admonitions* in its minimal use of colour, and in the noticeably thicker, heavier quality of the outlines – typical features of Song copies of earlier paintings.

Like the *Admonitions*, the *Benevolent and Wise Women* scroll is a pictorial illustration of a Confucian text about the cultivation and practice of virtue ethics by women of the elite. It illustrates a chapter from a book entitled *Biographies of Exemplary Women* composed by the imperial librarian Liu Xiang (77?–6? BC) in the late first century BC, towards the end of the Western or Former Han dynasty (206–7 BC). Indeed, some of the paragons in Zhang Hua's 'Admonitions' poem were borrowed from different chapters of Liu Xiang's *Biographies*. The extant *Benevolent and Wise Women* scroll depicts one chapter (it is not quite complete), but is the only surviving example from a set that was widely illustrated from as early as the first century of our era. Although *Benevolent and Wise Women* was made centuries after Gu Kaizhi's lifetime, it has been one of the major forces that shaped his historical image.

Both the *Admonitions* and the *Biographies* are concerned with ideals of feminine behaviour, and it is probably because of this common theme that another group of paintings, entitled *Goddess of the Luo River* and illustrating a romantic poem, has also been attributed to Gu Kaizhi for centuries. There are more than half a dozen scrolls in museum collections around the world illustrating the 'Ode of the Goddess of the Luo River', a romance composed by the poet Cao Zhi (192–232) recounting his liaison with a beautiful river spirit. One of these versions, *Goddess of the Luo River*, was acquired by the British Museum in 1930 as a companion piece to Gu Kaizhi's *Admonitions*. The example we illustrate here is the copy of Song dynasty date in the Palace Museum, Beijing (fig. 10).

On a long journey from the capital to his country estate, Cao Zhi spies a beauty that is invisible to other men. Discovering who she is, Cao Zhi begins to court her, but in the course of their encounters by the Luo River it transpires that the gap between the world of men and spirits cannot be bridged, and the affair ends, leaving the poet disconsolate. Most of these scrolls date to about the period of the Song dynasty, and were ascribed to Gu Kaizhi by connoisseurs from that time on, although it is now

9 ■ Attributed to Gu Kaizhi (*c.* 344–*c.* 406); Song dynasty
(960–1279). *Benevolent and Wise Women (Lienü renzhi tu).*
Handscroll; ink and light colour on silk, 25.8 × 470.3 cm.
Palace Museum, Beijing.

known the original illustration of the ode was a later, sixth-century endeavour. This makes sense if we consider how out of character a story about romance and desire – with no obvious ideological message – would have been in Gu Kaizhi's otherwise consistent oeuvre. Nonetheless, to artists and art lovers of the later dynastic period, these paintings were important visual evidence of Gu Kaizhi's art. At that time, having visual traces of Gu Kaizhi's painting overrode any concern with differences between types of painting of women – righteous and romantic – that today seem obvious.

There is one other aspect of Gu Kaizhi's art of concern here, his calligraphy. This arises out of the question of who was the calligrapher responsible for the calligraphic inscriptions in each scene of the *Admonitions* – if not Gu Kaizhi? In fact, this debate has more to do with the expectations and biases of late Ming dynasty (1368–1644) art critics such as Dong Qichang (1555–1636), who radically reshaped the tradition of literati painting, than the assessment of visual evidence from works ascribed to Gu Kaizhi or the historical sources. In the late Ming, any literati painter would have been expected to be a fine calligrapher as well as a painter, an expectation that was applied retrospectively into history. As a subject of the Eastern Jin dynasty, Gu Kaizhi, for his part, had lived in what the literati considered the founding era of self-expressive calligraphy. The Eastern Jin had produced the two best known calligraphers of all time, the 'Calligraphic Sage' Wang Xizhi (303–61) and his son Wang Xianzhi (344–88), known as the Two Wangs, who were the ancestors of the classical tradition of calligraphy. Traditionally, Wang Xianzhi's masterpiece was his transcription of Cao Zhi's famous ode in small standard script (fig. 11). As Gu Kaizhi was Wang Xianzhi's contemporary, the possibility that they had collaborated to make a single work of art – a *Goddess of the Luo River* picture-scroll containing the 'Three Perfections' of poetry, calligraphy and painting – was irresistible to Ming literati.

Judging from the surviving commentaries by Dong Qichang and others on the calligraphy of the *Admonitions* inscriptions, there must once indeed have been a tradition which held that the inscriptions to it were by Wang Xianzhi. However, critics including Dong Qichang went to great lengths to argue that the calligraphy was not by Wang, but by Gu Kaizhi himself. To prove Gu's interest in the art of calligraphy, Dong quoted a passage from Gu Kaizhi's biography stating that he was accustomed to 'burning the midnight oil' with his patrons discussing it. The late Ming literati's belief that the calligraphy was Gu's carried into the Qing period (1644–1911), but in

10 ■ Traditionally attributed to Gu Kaizhi (*c.* 344–*c.* 406); Song dynasty (960–1279). *Goddess of the Luo River.* Detail of a handscroll; ink and colour on silk, 27.1 × 572.8 cm. Palace Museum, Beijing.

the modern discipline of art history, a certain scepticism has arisen concerning the date of the calligraphy and, indeed, whether it was executed at the same time as the painting. Some scholars have argued that the inscriptions could have been inserted after the paintings, in the Song dynasty or later, for instance. In fact, the style of the inscriptions matches calligraphy of the late Six Dynasties period, which is contemporary with the painting style. The inscriptions were most likely done by a court calligrapher or scribe, working alongside the painter of the *Admonitions*, in an up-to-date (that is, fifth–sixth century), rather than Eastern Jin (fourth–early fifth century), style.

For many reasons, the attribution to Gu Kaizhi remains visually and intellectually compelling. The *Admonitions* scroll in the British Museum belongs to the category of Confucian narrative paintings, of which Gu Kaizhi is known to have painted many. This particular one is not mentioned in writing until 1103, when it was ascribed to Gu Kaizhi by Mi Fu in his *History of Painting* and lauded as one of the great early works of painting. While there are no surviving works by Gu Kaizhi, the *Admonitions* is more than simply a most important extant work of Six Dynasties painting. Based on the written evidence and from examining the painting itself, it was probably made closer

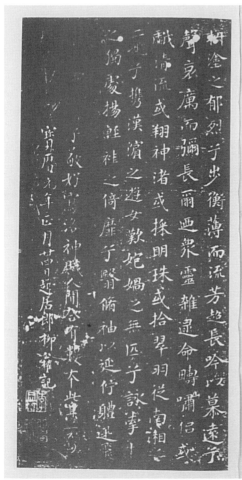

11 ■ Attributed to Wang Xianzhi (344–88). *Goddess of the Luo River Ode (Luoshen fu)*. Ink rubbing (Shi family of Yuezhou version).

to Gu Kaizhi in place, time and social-political context than anything else we know. It is an artwork of extraordinary richness and complexity, revealing the hand of an early master who was updating the classical style of Gu Kaizhi in the later Six Dynasties period.

2 | The *Admonitions* scroll scene by scene

The handscroll presenting a series of text passages accompanied by pictorial illustrations is a significant form of early East Asian scroll art. The *Admonitions* scroll is the prime example in the case of China; in Japan, a work of comparable importance would be the *Tale of Genji* picture-scrolls. Both deal with courtly subject matter; and in both cases the makers assumed their court audience already knew the text well. In these scrolls, the interplay of words and images created through collaboration between painters and scribes was both a real and a challenging way of telling the story or conveying a message, as it depended on the viewer's participation to create meaning. Knowing that the viewer was familiar with the basic story or admonition depicted enabled the artists to be selective rather than literal in their presentation of the material, and thereby to generate profound visual interest and, perhaps, challenging interpretations in their illustrations. In relating what is seen while viewing to one's personal knowledge and experience, the viewer – not the writer or the painter – becomes the real narrator of a picture-scroll.

The *Admonitions* owes its general format to the Han dynasty Confucian tradition of didactic narrative illustration: story-telling in word and image designed to reinforce values and ideology. But it also evinces exciting new developments in Six Dynasties pictorial imagery: an interest in aspects of daily life and the mundane, a heightened sense of the psychological and spiritual in portraiture, and a simple colouring method balanced against a lyrical outline technique comprising swirling rhythms and controlled hairline curves for painting drapery and figures. In combination with the subject portrayed, these aspects have the effect of compelling the viewer's interest and enriching the visual experience as he or she narrates the picture-scroll.

In fact, in early China of the Han and Six Dynasties period, courtiers might quite literally have felt they were living the narratives portrayed in the *Admonitions of*

12 ■ A palace lady at her toilette. Detail of the *Admonitions* scroll in the British Museum.

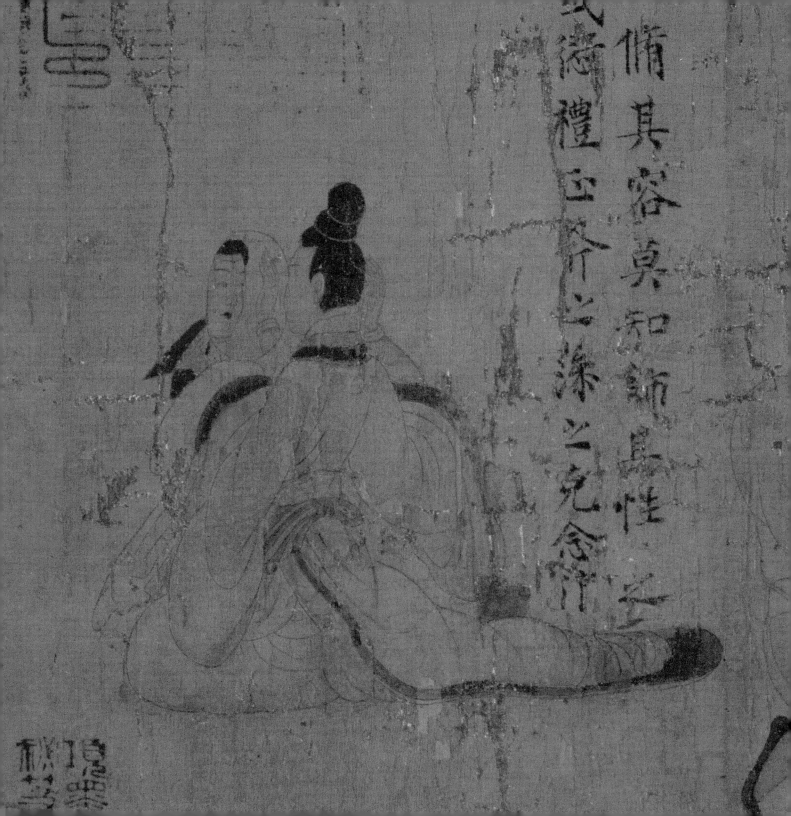

備其容莫知斯為性之
武德禮立容介之深之克念

13 ■ Song dynasty (960–1279) copy after Gu Kaizhi (*c.* 344–*c.* 406). *Benevolent and Wise Women.* Detail of a handscroll; ink and light colour on silk, h. 25.8 cm. Palace Museum, Beijing.

the Court Instructress. Scenes illustrating such stories were displayed in the living quarters of palaces of the imperial family (and the aristocracy), often on screens placed behind or beside where emperors and empresses sat. Ancient paintings and pictures themselves did not always show interiors or furniture, but those that do indicate how paintings filled the panels of screens placed behind important figures. In a scene on the lacquer-painted screen belonging to the Northern Wei courtier Sima Jinlong and his wife, a wife sits opposite her husband, who is surrounded by a three-panel screen. A similar scene appears in a painting attributed to Gu Kaizhi entitled *Benevolent and Wise Women*, which illustrates a chapter of Liu Xiang's *Biographies of Exemplary Women* (fig. 13). Intriguingly, this screen is painted with a misty riverscape – a clue that *Benevolent and Wise Women* was created in the Song dynasty when such landscapes were popular. (Painters often unwittingly 'update' styles and objects when making copies of ancient works.) The panels of day-beds and bedchambers provided a suitable format for such images, as is seen in another Song dynasty painting, *Night Revels of Han Xizai*, where again, the screens are filled with landscapes (fig. 19). However, we can still imagine how in early China when these panels were painted with stories of paragons of virtue, they acted as inspiration and caution to those who lived their lives among them.

Created in the Six Dynasties, a moment of cultural and political transition between the great Han and Tang empires, the *Admonitions* scroll exemplifies the earliest illustration of this didactic subject matter to be painted on silk in the more aesthetic form of a handscroll. In all its urbane wit, it reveals this friction between the old belief system and the new aestheticism.

As has been detailed in chapter 1, the rhyming poem illustrated in the *Admonitions* painting was composed in 292 by the courtier and savant Zhang Hua. Adopting the voice of a court instructress addressing her peers, he attempted to curb the outrageous conduct of the notorious Empress Jia. After becoming empress in 290, Jia dominated her recently enthroned husband, advanced members of her own clan without shame, and attacked enemies and rivals with a chilling ruthlessness. She quickly came to hold the strings of government, a flagrant violation of the expected role of a woman. Her schemes included plots to execute senior ministers and to frame and depose powerful members of the imperial family, including the heir to the throne, and the gruesome abortions of the unborn children of her rivals in the imperial harem. She is caricatured in the official history of the period as having been short and ugly, and a loose woman. Although politically-motivated plotting and assassination were not uncommon in that era, it was particularly shocking conduct for the figure of an empress. Jia caused scandal at court for more than a decade before she was finally deposed in a palace coup in 300 and forced to take poison. Zhang Hua met his death the same year after he refused to join the conspirators.

Although Zhang Hua was courtier to a weakling emperor and a tyrannical empress amid turbulent times, he did his utmost to maintain the stability of the dynasty he served. He was not a member of a powerful clan and the empress cannot have perceived him to be a threat. In fact, he owed his political comeback in the 290s to her. But in writing the 'Admonitions', he seems to have used whatever authority he had to try to remonstrate with her. His courageous intervention earned him the reputation of a loyal minister who dared to speak out against injustice when many others feared to, albeit with good reason: the consequences could be disastrous, not just for the minister concerned, but for his family and political allies. At the same time, having the conviction to speak out was one of the qualities a ruler most valued in his advisers, as not doing so could be ruinous for the entire state.

14 ■ Unknown court painter.
Breaking the Balustrade.
Northern Song dynasty, *c.* AD
1100. Detail of a hanging scroll;
ink and colour on silk, 173.9 ×
101.8 cm. National Palace
Museum, Taipei.

It was to reassure present and future ministers of his strong sense of justice that a Song dynasty emperor had a painting such as *Breaking the Balustrade* painted (fig. 14). It depicts a dramatic confrontation at the court of the Han emperor Chengdi (r. 32–7 BC) (the ruler whose palanquin Lady Ban refuses to share in scene 5 of the *Admonitions*). The noble hero holds the balustrade at the left demanding to be executed on the spot, while the obsequious villain cowers behind the furious emperor. Below, a man of upright character bows as he intercedes on behalf of the hero. The scene was intended to illustrate how officials should speak out against injustice, and that those who did could expect to be treated with respect by the emperor. An exemplar of this tradition of righteous remonstrance, Zhang Hua would probably have presented Empress Jia with his poem as a memorial to the throne. It seems he did not suffer for having done so, although the empress paid little or no attention to his admonition.

In adopting the persona of a court instructress, Zhang Hua voiced his concerns from within an existing literary genre about the conduct and virtue of palace ladies. This genre had emerged in the Han dynasty, a time when the Confucian *Dao* or Way was becoming rapidly institutionalized and Confucian virtue-ethics and mores of behaviour, including chastity, obedience and subservience on the part of women, were stressed. Compilations of model lives of women, such as the imperial librarian Liu Xiang's *Biographies of Exemplary Women*, appeared at this time, emphasizing the various accomplishments and worthy aspirations of womanhood. The virtue of filial piety, requiring respect and deference from social inferiors to their superiors, was the test of all human relationships, not just between father and son, and mother and daughter, but between siblings, married couples and, importantly, between the emperor and his subjects too. As well as being concerned with female virtues, Zhang Hua's 'Admonitions' poem is also similar to some Han dynasty prose-poems (*fu*) written by courtiers to emperors on the subject of imperial authority.

The 'Admonitions' poem opens with an introduction, which summarizes Confucian beliefs about the progress of human civilization since the time of creation, with emphasis on the role of women within the family structure. It concludes with the instructress closing off her lesson and presenting it to her audience, a type of 'autobiographical' statement conventional at the end of such texts and in early histories. Inbetween lies the body of the text, a series of cautionary tales and abstract precepts that make up the main message. The first four of these are historical anecdotes about ancient female paragons of self-sacrifice. As these tales had been illustrated since the Han dynasty, they would by Gu Kaizhi's time have been readily identified with standard compositional types.

The remaining six tracts are passages that describe in an abstract, poetic style how to perfect female virtue, and make use of the literary tools of rhythm and rhyme in the development of the ideas. These passages, however, had to be illustrated from scratch. Because of the abstract nature of the text passages, illustrating them would have presented a stiff challenge to any painter. Scenes 6–11 of the British Museum scroll show the painter to have latched on to any tangible thing mentioned on which to base his composition.

The content of the twelve 'Admonitions', and the corresponding illustrations in the British Museum scroll (parts 4–12) are summarized below. In the remainder of this chapter, we explore these images scene by scene. Our primary interest is in the London version of the *Admonitions*. This painting is today incomplete: it long ago lost scenes 1, 2 and 3 and the inscription to scene 4, perhaps through wear and tear as they would have been nearest the outside of the scroll. We therefore also make use of the Song dynasty copy of the *Admonitions* in Beijing to interpret the lost first third of the older, London painting.

1   Introduction: male and female, ruler and ruled. The role of women in Chinese civilization is to be 'submissive and meek' within the household.

2   Lady Fan: Lady Fan curbs her husband King Zhuang of Chu's excessive love of hunting by refusing to eat the flesh of the animals he killed for three years.

3   The Lady of Wei: the Lady of Wei ignores her own love of music to reform her husband Duke Huan of Qi's taste for licentious melody.

4   Lady Feng: Lady Feng selflessly steps into the path of an escaped black bear that has targeted her husband, Han emperor Yuandi, but is saved by armed guards.

5   Lady Ban: Lady Ban refuses to ride in the imperial palanquin for fear of making her husband, the Han emperor Chengdi, appear like a bad ruler.

6   The mountain and hunter: a mountain and a hunter with a crossbow about to shoot a tiger. An illustration of the couplet, 'To rise to glory is as hard as to build a mountain out of dust; To fall into calamity is as easy as the rebound of a tense spring.'

7   The toilette scene: two women are tending to their make-up and hair in illustration of the couplet, 'Men and women know how to adorn their faces, But there is none who knows how to adorn his character.'

8   The bedroom scene: seated on a canopied bed, an emperor and his concubine eye one another with suspicion to illustrate how false words will cause even your bedfellow to distrust you.

9   The family scene: several generations of a family sit together to illustrate the couplet, 'Let your hearts be as locusts And your race shall multiply.'

10   The rejection scene: an advancing beauty is rejected by the emperor: 'If by a mincing air you seek to please, Wise men will abhor you.'

11   A lady reflects upon her conduct: 'Fulfil your duties calmly and respectfully; Thus shall you win glory and honour.'

12   Conclusion: the court instructress. The court instructress writes out her admonitions for presentation to her peers, as two palace ladies approach her.

1 Introduction: male and female, ruler and ruled

From the chaotic cosmos were *yin* and *yang* separated;

From emanate force and amorphous form were they moulded and shaped.

With Fu Xi as ruler were the divine and the human distinguished.

Thus began male and female, the ruler and ruled.

The family's *dao* is regulated and the ruler's *dao* stabilized.

Feminine virtue honours yielding, holding within codes of moral behaviour;

Submissive and meek is the female's proper role within the household.

Having assumed matrimonial robes, she should reverently prepare the offerings;

Dignified and grave in deportment, be a model of propriety.

15 ■ 1: Male and female, ruler and ruled. Scene 1 of the Beijing *Admonitions* scroll. Song dynasty, 12th century. Palace Museum, Beijing.

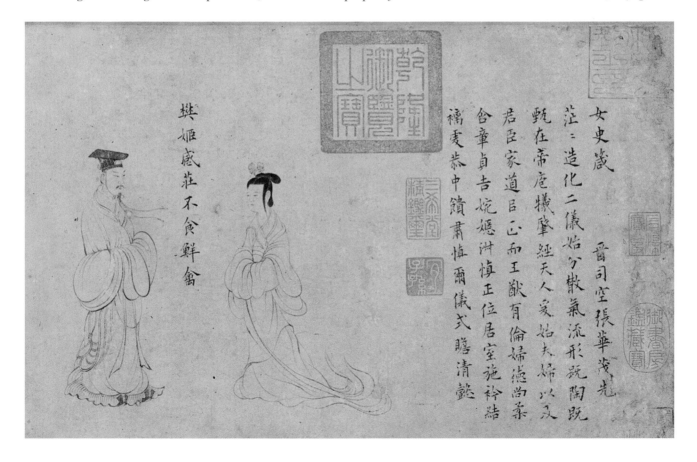

This scene being lost in the London painting, we consider here the Song dynasty version in Beijing (fig. 15). The painter of the Beijing *Admonitions* scroll chose to illustrate the opening of the scroll simply with two figures: a man and a woman, who stand facing one another in three-quarters view. They symbolize the *yin* (female) and *yang* (male) forces that in Chinese mythology separated out of the primeval chaos and gave form to the first people. Next, it is noted how the legendary ruler Fu Xi distinguished the divine from the human. Observing the markings on animals and forms of the earth, Fu Xi originated the Eight Trigrams of the *Book of Changes (Yi jing)*, the authoritative symbols with which mankind could establish communication with the divine, with Heaven. The emperor became the 'son of Heaven', and as long as he governed justly, received the mandate to rule from Heaven.

The two figures symbolize the two sexes that appeared following Fu Xi's distinction between divine and human. They also represent the 'natural', active-passive relationship between the sexes in classical thought: that man rules and woman is ruled by him. They show how the norm of the family was used as an image of the state. The male is the head of the family, and his wives are subservient to him, just as the emperor is the 'son of Heaven', and his subjects, like wives, are loyal and subservient. The emperor's wives, therefore, had a double responsibility as role models, both as wives in the imperial family and as model subjects in the emperor's larger family, the people.

This illustration of the scroll by a Song court artist identifies the continued importance of Confucian values in the later dynastic system. It was evidently still necessary to illustrate the most basic human relationship – between man and woman – to remind the scroll's viewers of their proper roles in feudal society. According to the text in this scene, a woman's role was to obey 'within the household' and, by implication, not to interfere in men's affairs of government and administration of society. The implication is that Song palace women were, like their predecessors, not always 'submissive and meek', 'dignified and grave', always looking to be of service. This apparently simple painting reinforces the stern warning in the text to the ladies of the imperial harem to be ever mindful of the consequences of their actions.

At first glance, this and the following two scenes of the Beijing scroll (that is, the missing scenes of the London version) do appear to have been copied from an original – and thus to preserve those lost compositions. But a closer look reveals the portrayal of human relationships and settings to be less complex and insightful on the part of the artist, when compared with the later scenes. Rather than their being copies, this suggests that the twelfth-century 'copyist' made them up by trying to imagine what an ancient painter would have done. He presumably had to do this because the front of the original scroll containing these scenes had already been lost. It is probable the British Museum's *Admonitions* had been parted from the opening section by about the end of the eleventh century.

The line of calligraphy falling between the man and woman in this scene is another indication of the lack of a clear model, for it properly 'belongs' to the next scene (about the vegetarian Lady Fan). In the British Museum scroll, the inscriptions are always placed immediately to the right of the illustrations. In the opening scenes of the Beijing scroll, however, the spacing of inscriptions and paintings was poorly plotted out, suggesting that there was a mix-up between the calligrapher and the painter as regards the layout. By rights, the single line inscription between these two figures should appear to the left of the man, as it refers to the following scene.

The copying of the ancient *Admonitions* is an example of one of the many projects glorifying Chinese culture and statecraft undertaken at the Southern Song court and geared towards showing that the native Song regime, and not the rival 'foreign' Jin dynasty (1115–1234) in the north, possessed the true mandate to rule China. The calligraphic inscriptions on the Song scroll also contain so-called taboo characters – the personal names of Song emperors that could only be written in somewhat altered form – which helps to date it to the twelfth century. Another important clue to a date after the eleventh century is the use of a plain outline without colour, a style that first became popular in early literati painting in the late Northern Song (960–1127), prior to the Jin invasion of the north.

2   Lady Fan

To influence King Zhuang of Chu, the Lady Fan ate no meat for three years.

樊姬感莊不食鮮禽

16 ■ 2: Lady Fan. Scene 2 of the Beijing *Admonitions* scroll. Song dynasty, 12th century. Palace Museum, Beijing.

Lady Fan was one of the wives of King Zhuang (traditionally r. 696–682 BC), ruler of the ancient state of Chu which lay in what is now central southern China. In ancient times Chu was known as an exotic and often terrifying wilderness. Disapproving of her husband King Zhuang's excessive love of hunting game in these southern forests, Lady

Fan tried and was famously able to reform him, by refusing to eat the flesh of the beasts he killed. By the first century BC, her story had made her a paragon of 'worthy and enlightened' female behaviour, appearing in a new book about women's deportment entitled *Biographies of Exemplary Women* (chapter 2) by the imperial librarian Liu Xiang. According to records, these biographies were soon illustrated in scrolls and on screens (long ago lost), and displayed in the imperial palaces as cautionary tales for the palace ladies.

In this Song illustration, Lady Fan kneels in profile a short distance away from a low table that has nothing on it. At the ends of the table stand three ritual food vessels that are patently *not* being used to cook or serve meat, in illustration of Lady Fan's three years of self-denial. The stemmed vessel is easily recognized as a *dou*, and the tripod as a *liding* – ancient bronze forms that the copyist thought a woman such as Lady Fan would have had at her disposal, and which conjured up a sense of the past in the scene for a later audience. In fact, such vessels are not depicted in early paintings, but this illustrates how far the Song dynasty craze for all things ancient, in particular bronzes and calligraphic inscriptions, had permeated this painter's mental image of the classical era.

From as early as the Han dynasty in China and more recently worldwide, bronzes have been seen as powerful representations of the longevity and sophistication of Chinese civilization. The most potent ruler of China during the Qing dynasty, the Qianlong emperor, for instance, valued the *Admonitions* scroll now in London above all other paintings in his enormous collection and called it a 'divine omen from antiquity'. (He also owned the Beijing version.) Referring to precious relics of the earliest dynasties, the Xia (unconfirmed) and Shang (*c.* 1600–1030 BC) bronze vessels, he also lauded the painting as 'the Xia tripod [*ding*] and the Shang wine-pot [*yi*] of precious paintings'. The Qianlong emperor knew that in myth, as no doubt in popular belief, only a true king of China – and never a tyrant – could obtain sets of ancient bronze vessels. For him, the appearance of the *Admonitions* scroll in his collection in the mid-1740s was as auspicious an omen as recovering a set of ancient bronze tripods.

3   The Lady of Wei

To reform Duke Huan of Qi, the Lady of Wei ignored her own love of music.
These two women's firm wills and lofty ideals changed the minds of two rulers.

17 ■ 3: The Lady of Wei.
Scene 3 of the Beijing
Admonitions scroll. Song
dynasty, 12th century.
Palace Museum, Beijing.

The Lady of Wei was a wife of Duke Huan of Qi (traditionally r. 681–643 BC), who
famously curbed his love of licentious music by her own self-denial. Like the story of
Lady Fan, the story of a woman from Wei appears in the chapter recording the lives of

'worthy and enlightened' paragons in Liu Xiang's *Biographies of Exemplary Women*. As in the case of the previous illustrations, without a model to base his composition on, the Song painter of the scroll invented a new one.

The Lady of Wei came from one of the two ancient states (the other was Zheng) renowned for licentious music, and she herself was a great musical talent. In the classical period, the names of these two states were even bywords for vulgar and degenerate arts in general, and classical texts are peppered with scornful references to their music. The thinker Xunzi complained that 'seductive looks and the songs of Zheng and Wei cause the heart to grow licentious'. The *Book of Music (Yue ji)* says that 'the tones of Zheng and Wei are tones in a world of chaos and compare to the dilatory ways of the people'. In the same book, a pupil of the sage Confucius, Zixia, remarks: 'Zheng tones are of a mind that tends towards doting excess and licentiousness ... Those of Wei are of a mind rushed and vexed.' Even Duke Huan's state music does not escape his criticism, as he goes on: 'Those of Qi are of a mind haughty and remote. All of these are excessive in their external attractiveness, and they are therefore harmful to one's virtue. For these reasons, they are proscribed from use in sacrifices and rites.'

Duke Huan of Qi was to find himself chastened by his wife's example, however, for as consort to the ruler of Qi, she refused to indulge either her own or his love of elaborate entertainment. To encourage the ruler to listen to the morally uplifting sounds of classical court music, she is illustrated not playing, but soberly listening to a performance by two musicians in thick black hats. One plays a set of bells and the other a set of stone chimes. Although sets of bronze bells similar to the one illustrated have been recovered from Zhou period tombs, it is to Song dynasty copies of ancient bells that these are most comparable (fig. 18). The weight and pitch of bronze bells in these sets were intended to set standards as well as practical systems (with cosmological underpinnings) by which sounds, weights, gauges and other measurements were

18 ■ Archaistic bell. Northern Song dynasty (960–1127), *c.* 1105. Bronze, h. 28.1 cm, w. 18.4 cm. National Palace Museum, Taipei.

regulated. They were also used to play music and establish rites by which the social hierarchy and social relationships were defined. In their turn, rituals, performances, dances and costumes were subject to elaborate state regulation and sumptuary law. Musical harmony, it was believed, would bring about cosmic harmony.

The Lady of Wei is pointedly listening to music which was part of a system of government designed to maintain stability and harmony in society and the state – rather than to the immoderate modern tunes that were said to be loud, complex and vulgar, and mixed the sexes in performance. The message of the story is that a woman who marries into a position of responsibility, such as the wife of a ruler, should use the example of her own behaviour to bring about self-improvement on the part of her husband where necessary, for the greater benefit of government and society.

19 ■ Attributed to Gu Hongzhong (*c.* 910–80); Song dynasty (960–1279). *The Night Revels of Han Xizai*. Detail of a handscroll; ink and colour on silk, 28.7 × 335.5 cm. Palace Museum, Beijing.

The story of the Lady of Wei had appeared in Liu Xiang's *Biographies of Exemplary Women* at a time of debate at the court of the Han emperor Chengdi about the use of modern or classical music at court. To the ears of Han conservatives like Liu Xiang, pleasing modern music was more than just a metaphor for lax morals, it actually caused the breakdown of social order. Musical propriety was no less important at the Song court, where there was a recurrence of the debate about legitimate ritual, music and instruments.

Belief in the power of music to precipitate virtue or debauchery, and hence transform or cause dissipation in society, underlay the official recasting of 'ancient' instruments such as the one seen in figure 18. It also left its mark in the cultural record in other ways, an example being the celebrated painting attributed to the Song artist

Gu Hongzhong entitled *The Night Revels of Han Xizai* (fig. 19). This painting illustrates just the type of behaviour that the Lady of Wei feared on the emperor's behalf, what in the Song would have been seen as un-Confucian conduct. This picture-scroll is said to be a record of the nightly entertainment and vice that took place at the house of Han Xizai, a prominent statesman and adviser to the emperor, made by a painter sent by the emperor to spy. In four pictorial movements the painting clearly illustrates how musical entertainment could be the prelude to more amorous pursuits. This is hinted at from the start, where, lying among the ruffled blankets of the bedchamber, we see the head and neck of a stringed instrument. However, the tale of the emperor's having commissioned the scroll leaves it unclear whether he was a Confucian moral rearmer or if he secretly delighted in the portrayal of these encounters – and the kind of 'sensuous' music that accompanied them.

4   Lady Feng and the bear

When the black bear escaped its cage, the Lady Feng hastened forward.
How was she not in fear? But, aware of mortal danger, she did not hesitate.

20 ■ 4: Lady Feng and the bear. Scene 1 of the London *Admonitions* scroll. The British Museum.

The British Museum *Admonitions* begins with the illustration of this story (fig. 20). The narrative formula repeated throughout the London scroll is one of text-inscription followed by picture-illustration. The loss of a large triangular area of the original silk in the lower-right corner of the picture (easily visible under ultraviolet light) suggests a missing section, which would have contained the inscription for this scene and the previous scenes.

The scene captures the drama of a series of true events that unfolded when a fearsome black bear escaped from the enclosure during an animal combat show put on for Emperor Yuandi (r. 48–33 BC) of the Han dynasty and a party of his favourite ladies from the imperial harem. In the illustration we see the beast, now on the loose, making for the emperor. The scene opens to two court ladies, companions to the seated emperor, who have turned to flee the approaching bear, but cannot prevent themselves from watching its progress with horror. Their reactions provide a clue to what we as viewers will shortly be feeling, if only we continue unrolling the scroll. Still with his legs crossed on a dais, the emperor, mouth and eyes wide open in shock, reaches for his sword to defend himself. Before him, confronting the bear, is the paragon of self-sacrifice, Lady Feng, who had the presence of mind to hasten into the bear's path when she saw it make for the emperor. To her great good fortune, two seasoned bodyguards have stepped in at the last moment, and are about to kill the animal, which rears up on one hind leg and snarls at them.

The description of the story in Zhang Hua's poem, however, mentions only the bare essentials of this event. It therefore becomes clear, as we explore the painting, that the painter had a much more detailed narrative in mind, one only alluded to in the two couplets of the poem. Lady Feng's moment of glory is recounted in the 'Biographies of Consorts' in the dynastic history, *History of the Former Han (Han shu*, chapter 97b):

> Lady Feng, like Lady Fu, was one of the emperor's favourites. In the Jianzhao era [38–34 BC], the emperor went to see an animal combat in the Tiger Enclosure. He and his concubines were all seated within the palace. A bear suddenly escaped over the fence. No sooner had the bear climbed the barrier and attempted to approach the palace than all the ladies, including the two at either side of the emperor and Lady Fu, ran away in panic. Only Lady Feng moved hastily toward the bear, and stood her ground in front of it. Then, two guards came quickly and killed the bear.

The retreating figure to the left of the bear, ignominiously thinking only to save herself, may now be identified as Lady Fu.

Throughout much of the *Admonitions* scroll's history, the 'missing' information needed to make sense of the painting would have been common knowledge among viewers. This knowledge would have been summoned up from memory with one's first

21 ■ 'Jing Ke attempting to assassinate the King of Qin'. Ink rubbing from a stone slab at the Wu Liang Shrine, dated AD 151. Jiaxiang, Shandong Province.

glance at the poem or painting. For the painter to assume that viewers would recall all the details of the story, including those omitted in the poem, was an obvious ploy to flatter their intelligence, and a way to lure them into the picture-scroll. But in this play between memory and image, the painter also enables his own narrative for the scene to unfold, as the viewer's attention soon shifts to the portrayals of the individual figures. The series of figures ends pointedly with the paragon of selfishness, Lady Fu.

Part of the vivid effect of this scene is the way that all the events portrayed appear to be occurring simultaneously – like a photographic snapshot. However, if we turn our attention to each individual we actually find that he or she is portrayed at the most dramatic or telling moment in his or her role within the story. Thus, the first two ladies are *about* to flee; the seated emperor is only *about* to reach for his sword; Lady Feng is *about* to be gored; the guards are *about* to save her; and Lady Fu, who has put considerable distance between the bear and herself, is *about* to be shamed. A modern equivalent is the film-making device in which a series of sequences from different perspectives, that supposedly take place at the same time, build up a single dramatic moment. This edited and somewhat conflated depiction of dramatic moments in a single 'simultaneous' scene is one of the distinctive story-telling devices of late classical–early medieval narrative illustration in China, as we know from the second-century engravings at the Wu Liang Shrine in Shangdong Province.

A particularly striking image there is the illustration of 'Jing Ke attempting to assassinate the King of Qin' (fig. 21). The designer of the scene conjures up the moment at which Jing Ke's righteous attempt to assassinate the tyrant has clearly failed. In the middle, his dagger has not reached its target – the alarmed King of Qin to the left – but become embedded in a pillar. A tassel attached to the haft is still horizontal in the air, about to fall. The would-be assassin, Jing Ke, whose hair stands on end, has already been detained by a guard. The sense of tragedy is palpable.

Like the illustrators of the Wu Liang Shrine, the artist of the *Admonitions* pinpoints the moments upon which human events turn — where glory is won or disaster befallen. In fact, political brinkmanship and life-and-death encounters in which individuals suddenly reveal their true colours were features of many court cultures in history, not just China's. Personal experience of this kind of event would have made the illustration of Lady Feng's dramatic story strikingly true to life for the emperors and court ladies who saw the *Admonitions* scroll. On the part of the artist, who was apparently a courtier himself, this was a very real way to try to convince them that their own fate, as well as the stability of the state, depended on their constant vigilance and integrity.

The story of the heroic Lady Feng is a popular one in both history and painting, and was illustrated in different formats such as intimate album leaves and handscrolls for study and leisure, as well as for display in the palace in wall or hanging scrolls. The basic pictorial formula required figures of the emperor and concubines, Lady Feng and the bear, guards and the cowardly Lady Fu. The lack of co-operation between the painter and the scribe that made the Beijing copy shows how much less dramatic the scene can be when the figures are widely spread; also, the inscription for the following scene cuts off Lady Fu (fig. 8). In later renditions, artists worked with this basic composition, and filled in the scenery according to conventions in use in their time. An album leaf probably by a Song or Yuan dynasty professional painter employs the original composition, but places the drama in a contemporary palace-garden setting, painted in rich red and green colour (fig. 24).

22 ▪ Ding Yunpeng (act. 1584–1618). *Lady Feng Confronts the Bear.* Handscroll. Palace Museum, Beijing.

In the late Ming dynasty, the eminent figure painter Ding Yunpeng (act. 1584–1618) painted *Lady Feng Confronts the Bear* in 1583 (fig. 22; Palace Museum, Beijing), in an elegant, Ming-style palace-garden setting. The distance the guards must cover to save Lady Feng makes the scene rather melodramatic, and the retreat of Lady Fu in the middle of the painting now becomes more understandable. In the mid-Qing, the Qianlong court painter Jin Tingbiao (act. *c.* 1727–d. 1767), whose patron owned both the London and Beijing versions of the *Admonitions*, illustrated the scene in a new composition in the hanging-scroll format, *Concubine Confronting a Bear* (fig. 23). This anodyne court painting shows neither the emperor nor Lady Feng to be in much danger — security is too tight for that, as 'two guards' have become two squads of guards. In a rewriting of history not untypical of the Qianlong emperor, the figure of the faithless Lady Fu quietly vanishes, no doubt to illustrate that no such sentiments as hers existed at the Qianlong emperor's court. Although this painting leaves little to the imagination, that is surely its point.

These works illustrate how different renderings of this scene in the later dynastic period (the Song, Yuan, Ming and Qing dynasties; 960–1911) could effectively stimulate or stifle social debate about virtue and

23 ■ Jin Tingbiao (act. *c.* 1727–d. 1767). *Concubine Confronting a Bear*. Hanging scroll; ink and light colour on paper, 150 × 75 cm. Palace Museum, Beijing.

Confucian ethics behind the story. What becomes clear is how the seeming continuity of a narrative illustration in fact shows up fundamental changes in the terms of that debate over time. Ding Yunpeng's painting in the late Ming dynasty coincided with a radical rethinking of the 'traditional' relationship between sovereign and subject, as the fading of imperial authority and a burgeoning market economy upset the old social order. In the eighteenth century, Jin Tingbiao's Qing court painting, by contrast, visually implemented the conservative Qianlong emperor's policy of restoring absolutist values, and shaped a perception of his court as a bastion of Confucian morality. A measure of the emperor's success is that throughout most of the twentieth century, students of the *Admonitions* were confused about the role and identity of the figure of Lady Fu in the London painting.

24 ▪ *Lady Feng and the Bear*. Song–Yuan dynasty, 12th–14th century. Album leaf (?); ink and colour on paper, *c.* 53 × *c.* 93 cm. The British Museum.

5   Lady Ban refuses to ride in the imperial litter

Lady Ban, by her refusal
Lost the pleasure of riding in the imperial litter.
Was it that she did not care to? No!
But she was anxious to avoid even hidden and remote consequences.

25 ■ 5: Lady Ban refuses to ride in the imperial palanquin. Scene 2 of the London *Admonitions* scroll. The British Museum.

After the single column of the inscription appears the beribboned figure of Lady Ban, wife of the Eastern Han emperor Chengdi (r. 33–7 BC). Seen in profile, she glides forward behind his litter, which is carried by eight bearers, who heave and strain under its weight, their faces set with grimaces and their arms and legs a commotion. Lady Ban's upright posture creates a striking contrast. Only her red scarf and two ribbons, fluttering out behind her as if blown by the wind, suggest movement. She looks straight ahead; her face wears no expression, although her hands are held open in front of her in a gesture that suggests self-righteous disdain. The emperor peers forlornly back at his favourite lady out of a window in the side of his transport. Beside him sits another court lady, whom he ignores. Again, it is assumed that the viewer knows the background to this story, as it is related in the *History of the Former Han* (chapter 97b):

> As Han emperor Chengdi was preparing to take an outing to the imperial garden, he invited Lady Ban to share his palanquin. But Lady Ban refused, saying: 'I have noticed that in ancient paintings wise rulers are always represented with their ministers at their sides, while decadent emperors at the close of the Three Dynasties have favourites with them. If I accede to your request, will you not resemble these latter?'

Even though this is not an important state occasion but a mere pleasure-outing, the virtuous Lady Ban refuses to accept the emperor's invitation to ride with him for fear of making him appear like one of the notoriously bad, last rulers of antiquity, whose pictures she has seen. The 'Three Dynasties' referred to the Xia, Shang and Zhou (*c.* 1030–221 BC) dynasties.

This is one of the scenes in the *Admonitions* that most clearly illustrates the sense of humour and the visual sophistication of its painter. Even though Lady Ban has made it clear to the emperor that he should devote himself to government and be attended by his ministers, he is pictured having replaced her with another of his court ladies. As all early viewers would have known, Emperor Chengdi's neglect of good government brought about the rise of the usurper Wang Mang and the replacement of the Eastern Han by the Xin (AD 8–24) dynasty. The painter shows how pointless Lady Ban's behaviour was: Emperor Chengdi found another companion and lost the dynasty anyway.

Where the same scene appears on the lacquer-painted Sima Jinlong screen (see p. 23), it is much simpler (fig. 26). Emperor Chengdi is not accompanied by another woman, and the scene does not generate the same level of visual immediacy in the manners and gestures of

26 ■ Story of Lady Ban. Lacquer-painted screen. Tomb of Sima Jinlong and his wife. Datong, Shanxi Province. Northern Wei dynasty, before AD 484.

27 ■ Mounted warriors. Detail of a mural in the tomb of Lou Rui (6th century). Northern Qi dynasty (550–77). Taiyuan, Shanxi Province.

the litter-bearers. There is also little sign of the subtle, unspoken communication between the emperor and Lady Ban that is seen in the *Admonitions*. What the screen image does indicate, however, is that this and similar scenes enjoyed wide visual currency in the Six Dynasties period in China, and were employed not only by painters of literary accomplishment in scrolls, but also by artisans working in the rather more humble media of lacquer, as well as probably clay and stone.

The litter-bearers in the *Admonitions* scene make a useful comparison with a group of warriors galloping on ponies in a sixth-century mural from the tomb of Lou Rui (fig. 27). The Lou Rui mural shows the new Western-influenced three-dimensional quality of the sculpted or painted figure at this time, described by critics as 'flesh'. While the palanquin-bearers have some of this corporeality, indicating a date for the *Admonitions* around that time, the silk-thread outline style harks back to the delicate lineament for which Gu Kaizhi was renowned in the fourth century.

Like the courageous Lady Feng, Lady Ban was well known in popular history in China, not only for her exemplary conduct, but also for her beauty. Along with Gu Kaizhi, she was one of the subjects selected by the eighteenth-century figure painter and print designer Shangguan Zhou to be included in his woodblock-printed anthology, *Painting Manual of the Hall of Old-age Smiles* (fig. 28). Beside a text detailing her accomplishments, she is portrayed in outline standing before the viewer as an upright, self-possessed woman. However, various details transform her into a model of mid-eighteenth-century Chinese beauty: a slightly rounded chin and delicate frame; the tasselled jade jewellery and patterned raiment; and the hair worn up in an elaborate coiffure.

The Lady Ban scene of the *Admonitions* also highlights a thorny issue over the last century concerning the 'authenticity' of the *Admonitions* scroll: whether the painting is an artist's original work or some kind of copy of that original. One common occurrence in the making of a copy, it is said, is the misunderstanding of certain 'passages' of a painting, often caused by a copyist's unfamiliarity with earlier fashions and customs, leading to mistakes in the copy that do not make sense visually. One often cited example is the rendering of the diagonal bars that hold up the frame over the palanquin that is draped with gauze. In the *Admonitions*, they do not meet this overhead structure at the corners, whereas in the Sima Jinlong screen they do.

If we take it that the artist wanted to paint the palanquin as accurately as possible – that is, as true as possible to the original structure he was representing – this would be a 'mistake' in the *Admonitions* scroll.

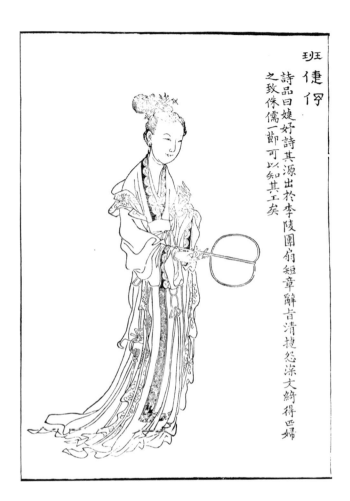

28 ■ Shangguan Zhou (1665–1749). 'Lady Ban', from the *Painting Manual of the Hall of Old-age Smiles*, 1743. Woodblock-printed book. Eighteenth-century edition. School of Oriental and African Studies Library, University of London.

29 ■ Detail showing repair and repainting to the scene of Lady Ban, in ultraviolet light. The London *Admonitions* scroll. The British Museum.

We may note, however, that even in the screen image of Lady Ban, the central support on the emperor's left has been moved to the right so that it does not pass across the figure of the emperor. In the British Museum painting, whether the rakish angles of the poles indicate that it is a copy by a copyist who got confused, or whether it is a feature of the original work by a careless artist, or indeed whether it results from some other factor altogether, has yet to be resolved. Recent ultraviolet photography of the scroll, however, suggests that much of the canopy is repainting carried out on an area of silk repair (fig. 29).

6   The mountain and hunter

In nature there is nothing that is exalted which is not soon brought low.

Among living things there is nothing which having attained its apogee does not
thenceforth decline.

When the sun has reached its mid-course, it begins to sink;

When the moon is full it begins to wane.

To rise to glory is as hard as to build a mountain out of dust;

To fall into calamity is as easy as the rebound of a tense spring.

30 ■ 6: The mountain and
hunter. Scene 3 of the London
Admonitions scroll. The
British Museum.

31 ■ Bronze censer in the shape of a cosmic mountain, *boshanlu*. Han dynasty. Palace Museum, Beijing.

To represent the warning issued to the Empress Jia and her clan in the first two lines, the painter literally illustrated each of the things mentioned in the last four lines. In the sky, as if borne along by clouds, are a red midday sun, containing a three-legged crow, and a white full moon, containing a rabbit or hare. We also see a mountain in the shape of a triangle. Game, wild beasts and trees appear all over it. There is also a tensed spring – a cocked crossbow in the hands of a kneeling hunter who aims at a tiger. The appearance of the 'tense spring' at the end of the scene visually reinforces the blunt warning about swift calamity in the admonition. A play on words adds further colour: in Chinese, the 'tense spring' puns on the 'scared pheasant' (*hai ji*). This is a literary conceit that would have made the illustration even more memorable for its intended early audience, as well as strengthening the link between the disproportionately sized hunter and mountain.

The earliest representation of mountains in China gave them this geometric form. Some Han incense burners were mountain-shaped, for instance (fig. 31); the smoke from the incense would recall rising clouds, an image of cosmic harmony and change. Wild animals were commonly depicted on these mountains, and were believed to be guardians of this intermediary realm between heaven and earth. The trees on this mountain are arranged in patterns: for the most part we see just repeated arcing tree tops rendered with a wiggly line and coloured in green. They generally appear behind the brows of the slopes, in a way that helps to define nearer from further-off chains of hills. The peaks that make up the mountain seem to be stacked diagonally each behind the last (see the right side). This repetition of pointed peaks is broken up by the flat plateaux on which they stand that fall away to steep cliffs.

It is not at all clear what all the masses and surfaces would actually correspond to in nature, probably because most of this highland scenery is actually repainting carried out on replacement silk support. Despite being added later, the texturing lines and shading give some indication of the original landscape style, although some areas, such as the part that appears to be strewn with rocks in the centre, seem beyond recovery.

The damage and repair to a large swathe of the mountain – ultraviolet photography shows only the lower-left area to be original – suggests this small landscape was the focal point of the painting during its later transmission, and that it was pored over by collectors and connoisseurs. This does tally with the much higher critical regard for landscape over figure painting by the Ming and Qing dynasties.

Although the trees seem to have been painted to the same scale as the mountain, the hunter, tiger, horse, pheasants and rabbit (or hare) all seem too large. However, to see this simply as a 'primitive' effect, practised at an early point in the story of painting at which painters had not fully mastered proportion, would be to miss other devices used to create meaning at work in the picture. An effective painter, after all, would be one that can create interest by manipulating the means of expression available at the time. Here, the painter took a literal, more holistic approach to illustrating the admonition. By choosing to include everything mentioned, as if his method were dictated by the text, a sense of overall pictorial realism got sacrificed – or perhaps it was not yet the overriding aim it is now assumed to be – in favour of a series of poetic images.

Illustrating a list of attributes or features in this way was actually a standard metaphorical device in early narrative painting. It appears in the *Goddess of the Luo River* scrolls, for instance. Although all the surviving versions of these are later copies, they preserve a composition that is close in date to the *Admonitions*, and until only recently was long believed to have been done by Gu Kaizhi. At one point in the poem, the increasingly love-struck prince-poet describes how he sees the goddess (she is invisible to others):

> Her body soars like a startled swan
> Gracefully, like a dragon in flight,
> In splendour brighter than the autumn chrysanthemum,
> In bloom more flourishing than the pine in spring;
> Dim as the moon mantled by filmy clouds,
> Restless as the snow whirled by driving wind.
> Gaze far off in the distance:
> She sparkles like the sun rising from the morning mists;
> Press closer to examine:
> She flames like the lotus flower topping the green wave.

32 ■ Traditionally attributed to Gu Kaizhi (*c.* 344–*c.* 406); Song dynasty (960–1279). The goddess from *Goddess of the Luo River*. Detail of a handscroll; ink and colour on silk, 27.1 × 572.8 cm. Palace Museum, Beijing.

In the illustration, all the various images and figures of her beauty are painted about her (fig. 32) as the story begins to stimulate the reader/viewer's desire and hope for fulfilment. The 'mountain and hunter' scene of the *Admonitions* is somewhat different in that it is a single lesson in a series designed to admonish, rather than part of a romantic but ultimately frustrating love story. In turn, the images in this scene illuminate the eternal cycles of nature – the rising and setting of the sun, the waxing and waning of the moon – as a prelude to sounding a warning note about greatness and the inevitability of decline. The mountain surely represents a great person, who has built it out of dust; but it is the cocked string of the hunter's bow that represents the speed and ease with which all this could be lost. They are, as it were, the carrot and the stick of the admonition: a representation of the reward for seeking virtue and sagehood, and an illustration of how fast 'calamity' would be triggered by not doing so.

7   The toilette scene

Men and women know how to adorn their faces,

But there is none who knows how to adorn his character.

Yet if the character be not adorned,

There is a danger that the rules of conduct may be transgressed.

Correct your character as with an axe, embellish it as with a chisel;

Strive to create holiness in your own nature.

33 ■ 7: The toilette scene.
Scene 4 of the London
Admonitions scroll. The
British Museum.

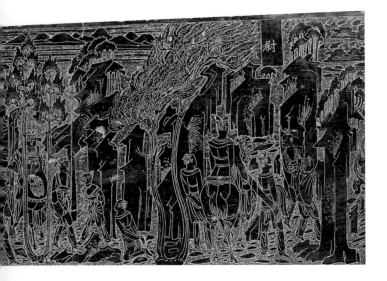

34 ■ 'Story of Wang Lin'. Detail of an engraved sarcophagus. Northern Wei dynasty (386–533). Nelson Gallery-Atkins Museum, Kansas City, Missouri.

Several palace ladies are at their toilettes. To the left, one lady kneels on a square, red-bordered mat, while another woman combs her long hair for her. They both look into a circular bronze mirror on a stand. The pole of the stand runs through a rectangular, mottled holder or tray. On the floor to their right are boxes made of black lacquer, one rectangular, two circular and tiered. The lid of one of the tiered boxes lies open on the floor, revealing its red lacquer interior; inside the open tier are small containers for the cosmetics. To the right, another kneeling lady, seen in three-quarters view from behind, makes a final check of her appearance. With her left hand she holds the mirror close to her face. Her right hand, which is reflected in the mirror, is poised in the air by the side of her face as she applies the finishing touch. The women's dresses in this scene are relatively simple in design.

The artist illustrated only part of the first line of the admonition, 'women know how to adorn their faces'; in fact, to wonder how he could have illustrated 'none knows how to adorn his character' may be precisely the point of this scene. The original text does not actually specify women – it says 'people', no doubt because men also wore make-up at this time. The artist chose to portray women in the inner quarters of the imperial palace to highlight what was wrong in the imperial harem. Once again, the painter uses an everyday event – putting on make-up – to suggest in terms of their own experience how much time the palace ladies spend on glamour, and how little on self-cultivation. They run the risk, therefore, of transgressing 'the rules of conduct' and not perfecting their inner natures. 'Adorning the face' is a warning of the necessity of 'correcting the character'; the mirror acts as a handy reminder that self-reflection should be more than skin-deep.

The mirror itself is an intriguing symbol, and has long been used in many cultures as an image of both superficiality and insight into truth. In medieval China, the image of the mirror often implied political or historical insight. In the early Tang dynasty, one of China's greatest rulers, Emperor Taizong (r. 626–49), was advised by a brilliant statesman, Wei Zheng (580–645), who was known as a 'mirror to the Son of

Heaven [the emperor]'. Paintings could also be mirrors of inner truth to their viewers. A founding work of painting literature, *Classification of Painters (Hua pin)*, by the Southern Qi dynasty (479–501) critic Xie He opens with the words: '… but of all who paint pictures there is not one but may illustrate some exhortation or warning, or show (the causes for) the rise or fall (of some dynasty), and the solitudes and silences of a millennium may be seen as in a mirror by merely opening a scroll.' The act of looking into mirrors here becomes a witty reference by the painter to his own art, as well as a claim to historical and political significance.

The image of the mirror was also employed as a poetic device in the 'palace-style' poetry popular in the Six Dynasties period, where it was used to conjure up the erotic but melancholy atmosphere of a palace lady's boudoir, where she anxiously awaits her inconstant lover deep into the night. A favourite subject in courtly fan paintings in China is indeed the love-sick beauty gazing into a mirror, lamenting the fading of youth and beauty. In this scene of the *Admonitions* painting, the artist cleverly combines these senses – of substance and transience. There is the positive moral idea that the viewer should 'reflect' upon the message, as he or she reflects upon his or her image. This sense of the mirror is playfully undermined by the associations with beauty and the boudoir. The stern message of the admonition is therefore tempered by the artist's aesthetic interest in glamour. Nonetheless, one could also say that by flattering the court ladies in his audience with these views of themselves as beauties, the painter guaranteed their attention to the subject at hand. The painting strikes a balance between creating a desirable self-image for these court women and encouraging their participation in the ideological system proposed in the 'Admonitions' text. The celebration of feminine beauty acts as a counterbalance to the doctrinaire tone of didacticism.

The unusual but intriguing composition suggests other levels of meaning within the scene. The lady on the right is a mirror image of the one on the left: they balance each other compositionally, and are seen from opposite sides. Also, the lady on the left is beginning her toilette, while the one on the right has just completed it, which suggests that she could be the same lady wittily portrayed in a manner of 'before/after' pictures. We can visualize the scene as rotating from left to right along an imaginary line down the middle of the picture. A very similar visual effect takes place in the story of the Confucian paragon Wang Lin on the roughly contemporary engraved stone

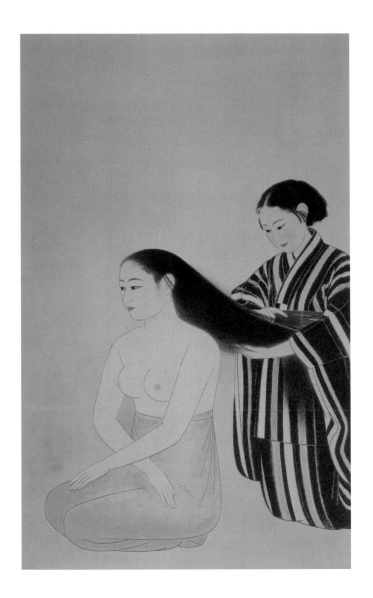

35 ▪ Left: Kobayashi Kokei (1883–1957). *Hair*, 1931. Ink and colour on silk, 174 × 108 cm. Collection of Eisei Bunko Museum, Japan.

36 ▪ Above: Kobayashi Kokei (1883–1957). Copy of the 'toilette' scene from the London *Admonitions* scroll, made in 1923. Collection of Tohoku University, Sendai, Japan.

sarcophagus in the Nelson-Atkins Museum of Art, Kansas City (fig. 34). That scene relates how after his brother is captured by bandits, Wang Lin offers his own life in his brother's stead (left half). Moved by his selflessness, the bandits let them go (right half). The party and rider approaching the viewer on the left, as Wang Lin's brother is about to be executed, have 'swung' through the picture plane around the pair of trees in the middle, so that on the right everyone is seen leaving from behind.

In the Wang Lin scene, this mirroring or pivoting device is used to illustrate Wang Lin's virtue being put to the test (left) and his immediate reward (right). This is a transformation that can hardly be depicted in form, but it can be suggested via a pictorial device that tells of a pivotal moment. The toilette scene may be read in the same way. Rather than being just about the appreciation of womanly beauty, however topical that may have been, or just an image conveying the admonition to correct one's character 'as with an axe', the scene becomes more interesting with the addition of layers of meaning, as if it were visual poetry.

The 'toilette' scene was one of those copied by the Japanese master of Nihonga painting, Kobayashi Kokei (1883–1957), on his visit to the British Museum in 1923 (fig. 36, to which we return in the final chapter). Kokei's copy was later taken back to Japan where it has since been in the keeping of Tohoku University in Sendai. Images of women at their toilettes were common in the Japanese woodblock-print tradition. However, the composition, the outline drawing technique, the modulated and 'block' uses of colour, and the facial expressions and beauty of the women in this ancient example of a familiar scene evidently made a deep impression on Kokei. In 1931 he reused the left half in a new painting of a Japanese domestic scene entitled simply *Hair* (fig. 35). In *Hair* the two women now face left, with the seated woman looking into a mirror out of the picture. Using an even closer viewpoint, *Hair* seems to delight in the evocation of female beauty with the subtle modulation of pink tones throughout the painting, as well as the play of straight and curved lines to render both women's faces and the upper body and arms of the woman seated.

8   The bedroom scene

If the words that you utter are good,
All men for a thousand leagues around will make response to you.
But if you depart from this principle,
Even your bedfellow will distrust you.

In a daring composition set right in the heart of the inner palace, the emperor is paying a visit to a lady of his harem in her bedchamber. If what you say is good, the admonition relates, everyone about you will respond to you. But if your words deceive, even your lover or bosom friend will become suspicious of you. The body language and expressions of this couple tell a story of distrust between them. The emperor sits on the edge of the bed, where he has tarried some time, for his left foot is crossed by his thigh and his right foot is inserted absent-mindedly inside his shoe. His upper body and head are turned towards the lady in the bedchamber. He gives his lady a supercilious look, and there is the suggestion of a frown on his brow. The back of the bedfellow, who sits opposite dressed in a red shirt, is pressed up against the panels of the screen around her bed, as she pushes herself into the furthest corner. Her right arm is held awkwardly outside the screen and her armpit rests on top of it, as if she were squeezing it for support. Her face, seen in sharp profile, is set with a hard look of anger or hostility. Between their faces, symbolic of the mistrust that has arisen between them, a blade-like swathe of black cloth hangs down from the canopy of the bed.

The painter's choice to illustrate the text with a bedroom scene is not just risqué but also politically apt. Literally, it refers to the emperor's relations with the women of his harem, who he visits in the back palace for his own pleasure and the procreation of heirs. It is more than just a titillating scenario, however, as the image of 'getting into bed' with someone was a metaphor for creating alliances or casting in your lot with another person which was most topical in Six Dynasties political life. To maintain their grip on power, the leaders of court factions were often obliged to ally themselves with other equally ambitious and often unscrupulous rivals. A courtier-painter, be he Gu Kaizhi, who served at court and as aide-de-camp to several of the leading politician-generals, or a later master working in his style, would certainly have had first-hand experience of such deals and of the often bloody consequences when one party double-crossed another. In the artist's punning interpretation, the appeal of the scene is wittily broadened to include not just the women of the imperial harem, but the men and women of the court at large.

Despite the profound psychological interest of these figures, evoked through control of the media and imaginative input of the painter, there are a number of 'mistakes' as far as the drawing in this scene is concerned. The multi-legged table, for instance, was a fairly common medieval design (see the cave mural of Vimalakirti in

37 ■ 8: The bedroom scene. Scene 5 of the London *Admonitions* scroll. The British Museum.

38 ■ Swathed bedchamber.
Rubbing of a stone engraving.
Northern Wei dynasty
(386–533). Tenri University
Museum, Nara, Japan.

fig. 4), but the legs at the far end of this table are misplaced in some way and are not at the end of the table. Curiously, the screen around the chamber comprises only two panels at the far end of the bed, whereas there are three at the near end. The panel hiding the emperor's body has been made narrower than the rest so as to show part of him. The long rear ridgepole of the canopy has wandered nonsensically up to the left, making the canopy hopelessly out of proportion with the chamber below.

Much of the silk medium on which the scene is painted is in poor condition and there is evidence of substantial repair work, so it is possible that these errors may have been inserted at a later date by a restorer who was unfamiliar with the furniture and design characteristics of medieval times. The swathed design of the bedchamber itself was common in the Six Dynasties, and similar examples of these chambers are seen in tomb murals of the period (fig. 38). Executed by artisan-painters, these are fairly crude, but do show the 'correct' form of the furniture.

9   The family scene

To utter a word, how light a thing that seems!

Yet from a word, both honour and shame proceed.

Do not think that you are hidden;

For the divine mirror reflects even that which cannot be seen.

Do not think that you have been noiseless;

God's ear needs no sound.

39 ■ 9: The family scene. Scene 6 of the London *Admonitions* scroll. The British Museum.

40 ■ Edouard Manet
(1832–83). *Le déjeuner sur l'herbe*, 1863. Oil on canvas, 214 × 269 cm. Musée d'Orsay.

Do not boast of your glory;

For heaven's law hates what is full.

Do not put your trust in honours and high birth;

For he that is highest falls.

Make the 'Little Stars' your pattern.

Do not let your fancies roam afar.

Let your hearts be as the locusts

And your race shall multiply.

The text of this scene is a long admonition about the need to maintain constant vigilance over one's thoughts and actions, in public and particularly when alone, and about virtue (rather than superficial titles and rewards) as the absolute yardstick by which character and conduct are judged. Only the last two lines, which allude to locusts in the classics, seem to have offered the painter much possibility for his composition, for he chose to illustrate a family scene showing the happy growth of the imperial clan.

The painter creates immediate visual interest by presenting his figure group in a geometric form – a triangle. Such a form does not appear in nature; nor had it appeared in pictures until this time. To the modern eye the use of this shape is hardly radical, being familiar from paintings of Renaissance Europe, as well as from Edouard Manet's (1832–83) *Le déjeuner sur l'herbe* of 1863, for instance, where it is understood to have been a parody of classicism because of the 'vulgar' contemporary figures within it and its idyllic setting (fig. 40). In the case of the *Admonitions* scroll, in the context of early didactic narrative painting, the use of this shape was wholly novel and refreshing, and offers an interesting visual counterpart to Zhang Hua's admonition in this scene. Within the scroll, this triangle immediately recalls the pyramid form of the mountain a few scenes earlier. There, the shape connoted stability and greatness and these ideas are surely to be inferred from the appearance of the same shape here. This makes sense as the message of the admonition is that palace women should aspire to breed 'like locusts' for the posterity and continuing glory of the ruling household.

Stylized forms and movements, not to mention the schematic shapes of the figures and the play of delicate thin lineament across the surface of the silk recur through the *Admonitions*. Outwardly, the triangle symbolizes stability, but there are evident psychological tensions between the individuals within the form, as in other scenes by this sanguine painter. In the lower right kneels the emperor, whose figure is larger than all the others. In part, his size may be a hangover from early painting in which figures of higher status were painted larger than their subordinates, as seen in funerary depictions of the deceased in Six Dynasties tombs. But the emperor here also appears to be the closest to the picture plane/viewer, which is to say that the painter has used foreshortening to give the illusion of spatial recession.

Despite the emperor's dignified posture and straight face, which were conventional for such figures, he is holding something behind his back in his left hand – a toy, perhaps that he is hiding from one of the children. To his right sits one of his wives in a red chemise. She holds out a red pom-pom ball on a string with one hand and beckons with the other as she tries to distract the little boy in red dungarees. His face is a tale of woe as he is going through the unpleasant business of having his hair combed by another lady opposite. To the left are two smaller children with their hair tied in playful tails. One sits on the lap of a beauty, who wears a white dress with red trim, while the other scampers on the floor. The emperor and lady to his right glance down at the children, while the lady in the front left looks directly at the emperor. These gazes make tense connections run between the figures on each side. As the viewer follows these movements within the painting, the scene becomes more than just a family group, but the telling of a story within it in relation to the text to the side.

Some way behind them, at the top of the triangle, is a third group. These figures are both smaller and 'tucked' behind the heads of the ladies at the front to suggest that they are sitting on the same floor, some distance back. We may imagine the ground rising diagonally back into the picture. In the centre of the group an old man in a red cap holds out a scroll teaching a girl to his left and a younger boy to his right, both of whom hold orange-backed scrolls. The teacher's eyes are turned askance towards his female pupil who seems to be stumbling in her reading of the lesson.

At first glance the pyramid shape of the assembled family suggested stability and permanence, but as the viewer's attention shifts to individual groups within the triangle, to the individual peaks that together make up the mountain, a distinct change of mood takes place. The eye moves from children to adults to an old man and back: now the transience of past, present and future generations is mooted.

10   The rejection scene

No one can please forever;
Affection cannot be for one alone;
If it be so, it will end in disgust.
When love has reached its highest pitch, it changes its object;
For whatever has reached fullness must needs decline.
This law is absolute.

41 ■ 10: The rejection scene.
Scene 7 of the London
Admonitions scroll. The
British Museum.

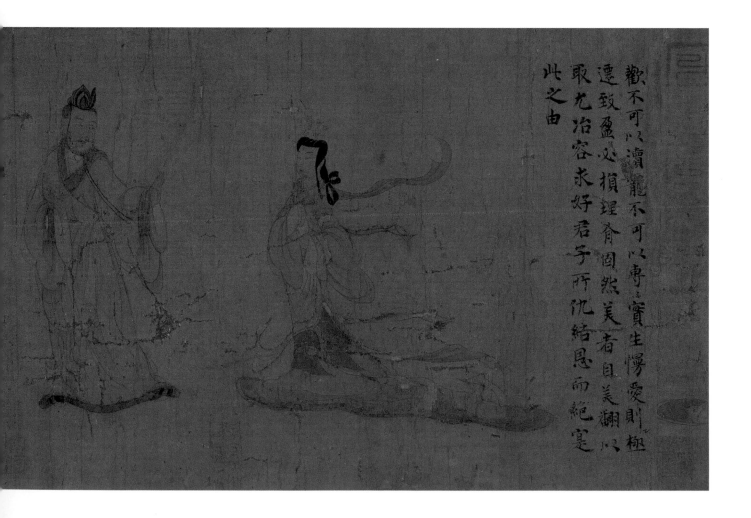

The 'beautiful wife who knew herself to be beautiful'
Was soon hated.
If by a mincing air you seek to please,
Wise men will abhor you.
From this cause truly comes
The breaking of favour's bond.

The 'beautiful wife who knew herself to be beautiful' has advanced upon the emperor, who, with his eyes fixed hard upon her face, unequivocally halts her approach with his outstretched hand. The first suggestions of affront at his rejection are appearing on her face. She has come upon him fast: the ribbons and train of her dress stream out behind her. But now her shoulders are arched back a little awkwardly and her arms are quickly being gathered up towards her nape – as if she were preparing to make an abrupt halt. Although her face has an expression as if 'butter would not melt in her mouth', her gaze is somewhat downcast; her mouth gives the hint of a sullen pout. For his part, the emperor appears to have been rocked back in surprise, for his feet are still planted to the floor as his torso turns away to the right. As he gestures his revulsion at her 'mincing air' with his hand, he prepares to turn on his heel to leave in disgust. On his face, what moments ago may have been a look of affection has become a look of disappointment and pity.

Within a slightly off square composition, the painter uses the figures' gazes and gestures and the play of their clothing to create a kind of zigzag movement between them, as if narrating the series of unspoken communications that is taking place. The emperor's eye fixes hers. She glares at his outstretched hand, which itself is directed towards her body and its forward momentum. Both figures appear to teeter back in opposite directions. A permanent distance is about to come between them as we witness the actual moment of 'the breaking of favour's bond'.

Like the pleasurable music of the states of Zheng and Wei, seductive looks were, in Confucian doctrine, a cause of the heart growing licentious. In the scene depicting the Lady of Wei, this

42 ■ 'Lady and dragon'. Painting on silk from a tomb at Changsha, Hunan Province. 3rd century BC.

43 ■ Two beauties from 'The Story of Shun'. Detail of an engraved stone sarcophagus. Northern Wei dynasty, early 6th century. Nelson-Atkins Museum, Kansas City, Missouri.

precept could be illustrated using the musical metaphor. Here, however, much of the admonition text presents abstract ideas that would have been tricky to illustrate. The first five lines, for instance, echo the idea in the scene of the mountain and hunter that the forces of nature including favour and affection, ebb and flood, like tides, or seasons or phases of the moon. Chinese emperors had many wives in the harem; only the emperor, female servants and eunuchs had access to the 'back palace', in order to ensure the integrity of the dynastic line. The emperor was meant to 'favour' all his wives and concubines, and none was meant to monopolize his affections to safeguard the stability and posterity of the dynastic house. It was not that sexual or any other kind of pleasure – such as the enjoyment of wealth, titles, privileges, and so on – was considered wrong. On the contrary, these were the just rewards for upright behaviour. Rather, an overly strong bond with one individual could cause the ruler's impartial judgement to become partial or his balanced conduct to become skewed. In this scene, the beautiful wife has hoped to take advantage of his affections, which is immediately abhorrent to her 'wise man'. The message of this scene is directed as much to men as to women. A minister's relationship with a ruler should also not become overly close.

The model of beauty with the hour-glass or 'stem-ware' figure exists in painting as early as the Han dynasty, in a silk painting depicting a woman and a dragon from a tomb in Changsha, Hunan Province (fig. 42). A more contemporary example of beauty is found in the figures of the legendary sage-king Yao's two daughters as they are presented to Yao's worthy successor, Shun, in a 'filial piety' scene on the Kansas City sarcophagus (fig. 43). The same scene also appears on the laquer screen in Sima Jinlong's tomb (fig. 7). A clever and ironic touch in the *Admonitions* 'rejection' scene is the way the artist playfully mocks the conventional link – seen in the engraving and lacquer painting – between outer beauty and inner virtue.

11   A lady reflects upon her conduct

Therefore I say, be watchful: keep an eager guard over your behaviour;
For thence happiness will come.
Fulfil your duties calmly and respectfully;
Thus shall you win glory and honour.

To illustrate this admonition, the painter portrays a single court lady kneeling in a state of introspection, reflecting upon her duty and conduct, upon how to 'win glory and honour'. Her mouth is set in a rather firm expression, and her eyes gaze very slightly downwards at a point some way in front of her. There is a sense of self-restraint about her, which is created by the contrast between the stillness of her pose and the signs of inner emotional activity suggested by her facial expression and the fluttering ribbons of her dress. This penultimate scene is important to the visual plotting of the entire scroll, for in the use of a stable, pyramidal shape for the figure it creates a moment of calm before the last flourish and closure of the final scene. This scene, at least, seems to work as a moment to focus introspectively on all the foregoing examples, a step before announcing the conclusion of the piece.

The evident difficulty with which this court lady is attending to the admonition provides a model of dutiful behaviour that is all the more convincing for being rather troubled. Had she been the perfect lady, one suspects, she would have appeared most unrealistic, and perhaps even comic, to early court viewers of the work. This brings us back to the question of just what the intention of the painter was in illustrating a Confucian didactic text about female conduct at court. Whether we consider the painter an ideologue who was sympathetic to the message of the text or not, he uses a variety of persuasive techniques to draw out the lessons. The great beauty and attraction of the female figures would surely have generated interest by flattering female viewers and arousing male ones. The realistic portrayals of the difficulties involved in being good suggest an insightful mind and a dry wit.

44 ■ Previous page:
11: A lady reflects on her
duty. Scene 8 of the London
Admonitions scroll. The
British Museum.

12   The instructress

Thus has the Instructress, charged with the duty of admonition
Thought good to speak to the ladies of the palace harem.

An elegant court lady stands slightly stooped towards a scroll, held in her left hand, on which she writes with a brush, held in the traditional posture in her right. She wears on her face an expression of good-natured concentration. She is approached by two court ladies, who appear to glide towards her from the direction of the end of the scroll, as the trains and ribbons of their dresses flutter out behind them. The lady furthest

45 ■ 12: The instructress. Scene 9 of the London *Admonitions* scroll. The British Museum.

away in the picture plane, gesturing with her hands spread open and apart, turns her head as if to speak to her companion. Their conversation is clearly about the 'Admonitions', for the eye of this second lady, who is seen in profile, is fixed upon the open scroll across from her. Her rouged lips curve upward in the slightest of smiles; her posture suggests the slightest stiffening of her back at the prospect of criticism. Her face wears a look of inner calm, but her body language and gaze, and even the light

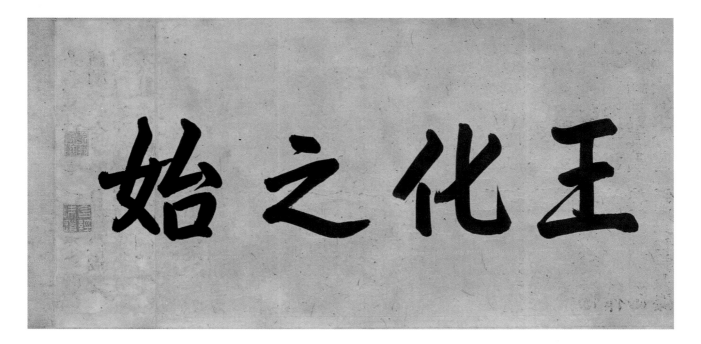

46 ■ 'The beginning of kingship' *(wanghua zhi shi).* Title-piece by the Qianlong emperor (r. 1736–95) to the Song copy of the *Admonitions* scroll. Palace Museum, Beijing.

ruffling of her ribbons in an imaginary breeze suggest otherwise. The instructress is recording the foregoing admonitions in writing for presentation to her peers for their self-improvement. These two women have happened upon her as she concludes her work, at the same time as the viewer completes a reading of the scroll. Their emergence from left, the opposite direction from which the scroll has been read, is the pictorial counterpart to reaching the end of the text.

The figure of the court instructress that Zhang Hua employed as the author of his admonitions is described in the ancient *Book of Poetry (Shi jing)*, one of the Chinese classics (the canonical texts about rites, music, history and poetry). There it is said that 'In antiquity, a female courtier was selected from among the palace ladies to carry a red tube, (meaning that she was charged with the duty of) recording the transgressions of her fellow concubines for their own instruction.' Beginning in the Han dynasty, there have been different interpretations as to what the 'red tube' actually was and how it was used to admonish, ranging from a painted or varnished lady's trinket that was presented to miscreants, to a flute (that was played to them), to a writing brush used to commit their faults to writing.

Here, the painter illustrates the 'red tube' as a brush. Although this might seem the obvious interpretation, a high degree of literacy did not actually become one of the standard accomplishments of the elite until the Han dynasty, when – with new technology – paper and the writing brush first began to be widely used. In the period corresponding to the opening centuries of the Christian era, early artists began experimenting with the new possibilities afforded by these highly flexible new media. It was only by about the fourth and fifth centuries that works of calligraphy and painting by learned gentlemen as well as ladies – rather than nameless artisans – began to be treasured, and 'art collections' of them formed.

The illustration of the instructress concluding her admonitions text provides a pleasing explanation for the existence of the scroll itself. It was the virtue of this classical figure of the court instructress that the Qianlong emperor alluded to in his title-piece to the scroll, which reads 'fragrance of a red tube' (*tong guan fang*; fig. 66). His title-piece to the copy in Beijing conveyed his understanding of the *Admonitions* as 'the beginning of kingship' (*wanghua zhi shi*; see fig. 46). The emperor also painted a single spray of wild orchid on one of the silk border-panels of the London scroll 'to accord with the idea of chaste beauty' in the *Admonitions* paintings (fig. 47).

47 ■ A 'lonely orchid', painted by the Qianlong emperor (r. 1736–95) on one of the silk border-panels inside the *Admonitions* scroll. The British Museum.

3 | The calligraphy in the Admonitions

In evaluating the date and place of the *Admonitions* in history, it is important to consider not just the relationship between the text and painted images, but also the pictorial sophistication and the lyricism of the lineament, the silk medium and ink and colour pigments, and indeed the historical records. We also need to take into account the calligraphy – the writing style and authorship of the inscriptions that accompany each painting (fig. 48). They are as much a part of each scene as the images, and were certainly as important as the images to the scroll's owners and viewers over the last millennium. During that time the art of calligraphy in China was a vital cultural paradigm, as indeed it remains today.

In dynastic China, calligraphy was believed to embody signs and energies of the cosmos, and trying to understand these by practising calligraphy was a path to self-cultivation. In myth, the first graphs were impressions of birds' feet in soft mud which were recognized as cosmic signs by the legendary ancient sages, Fu Xi and Cangjie. Pictographs and then ideographs increased in number and thereafter developed into a fully-fledged written language. Historically, writing begins in China with early Shang dynasty divination texts on bone; and soon after, 'seal' script appears on ritual bronze vessels. Writing tools became more sophisticated, changing from awls to styluses, and, around the Han dynasty, to brushes – the tool with which Han 'clerical' script was written.

By the seventh century, all the basic scripts – including seal, clerical, cursive and block or regular script – were complete, and a classical tradition had been established. Also known as the Wang tradition, after the Calligraphic Sage Wang Xizhi and his son Wang Xianzhi, it held that 'the calligraphy is the man': an elegant, expressive hand was the visual trace of an individual's inner values, and Wang Xizhi was the prime exemplar of this tenet. Indeed today, the masthead of the *People's Daily* news-

48 ■ The rejection scene, detail of the calligraphic inscription. The *Admonitions* scroll. The British Museum.

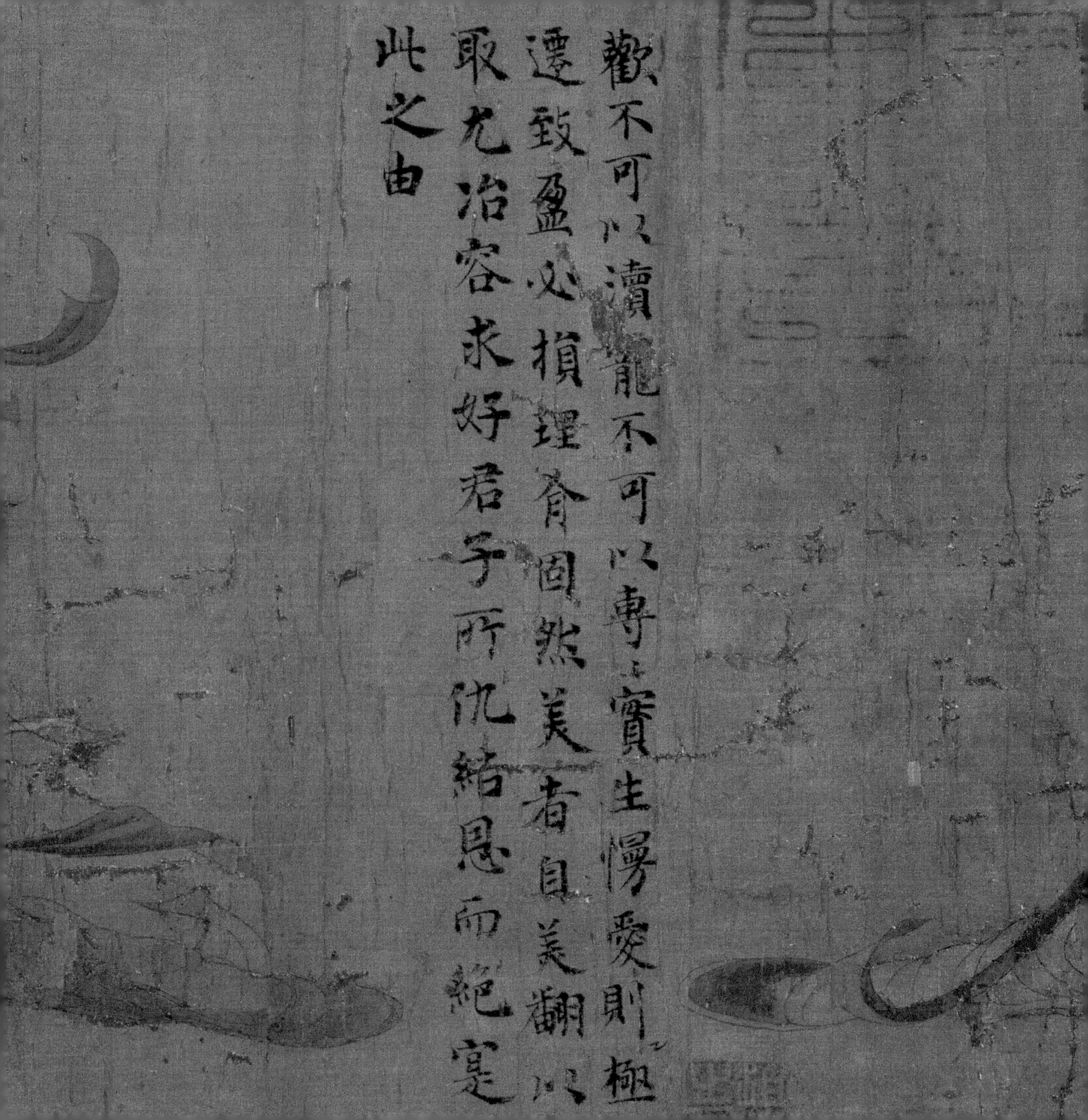

歡不可以瀆寵不可以專實生慢愛則極
遷致盈必損理育固然美者自美翩以
取尤冶容求好君子所沈結恩而絶寔
此之由

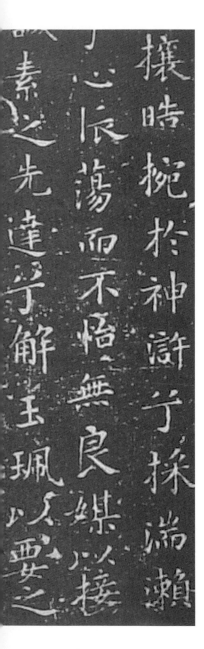

49 ■ Wang Xianzhi (344–88).
*Thirteen Lines of the Goddess of
the Luo River Ode*. Ink rubbing.

paper, the mouthpiece of the Chinese Communist Party, is printed in the calligraphy of – and hence draws authority from – the late Party Chairman Mao Zedong (1893–1976).

The use of calligraphic style has long been exploited by patrons and artists to promote ideas and values, but also to write social commentary and satire. Following the appearance of a new social class of scholar-officials – or *literati* – by the eleventh century, the art of calligraphy became increasingly associated with the sister arts of poetry and painting. Together, they were called the Three Perfections: poetry, calligraphy and painting. That they were the three principal modes in later Chinese art illustrates the significance of personal or *lyric* expression in Chinese aesthetics.

Part of collectors' fascination with the *Admonitions* over the last millennium lies in its being an early example of a scroll containing the Three Perfections: the poem by Zhang Hua, the calligraphy, and the painting by Gu Kaizhi. In the eleventh century, connoisseurs no doubt assumed the calligraphic inscriptions had been penned by Gu Kaizhi, who was a gifted man of letters as well as a painter. However, by the late Ming dynasty, the authorship of these had become a point of contention among leading connoisseurs. Some doubted the calligraphy was by Gu Kaizhi, whose painting and not his calligraphy had been treasured through history, in which case it could only have been by Gu's great contemporary, the calligrapher Wang Xianzhi. Wang Xianzhi was famous for his transcription in small standard script of the poet Cao Zhi's 'Goddess of the Luo River Ode' (fig. 49), which was part of the classical canon of calligraphy. As a painting subject, the ode was of course synonymous with Gu Kaizhi. Now, the combination of three great talents in Zhang Hua, Wang Xianzhi and Gu Kaizhi on the production of the *Admonitions* scroll was, similarly, an intriguing possibility to Ming literati. By contrast, through much of the twentieth century a prevailing scepticism in connoisseurship of Chinese pictorial art meant that scholars were prepared to link the *Admonitions* painting closely with Gu Kaizhi, but were doubtful about the authorship of the inscriptions. We will consider further what connoisseurs have historically thought of the calligraphy in the next chapter, but turn first to our own dating of it.

For the most part, the text as inscribed on the scroll is easily read aloud: one does not need special training to be able to recognize or sound out these characters in modern pronunciation. Understanding the sense, however, requires some knowledge of classical Chinese poetry, as the language is not punctuated with full stops and commas, but by words, conventions and rhymes (in ancient pronunciation), and meaning. If one simply intones the characters aloud in modern Chinese one may easily misconstrue the poetry.

Let us take as an example the calligraphy of the 'rejection' scene, lines 63–74 of the poem. The inscription is three and a quarter lines long, and is preserved in relatively good condition. It may be read in modern Chinese and translated into English as follows:

63. 驩不可以黷
huān bù ké yǐ dú
No one can please forever;

64. 寵不可以專
chǒng bù ké yǐ zhuān
Affection cannot be for one alone;

65. 專實生慢
zhuān shí shēng màn
If it be so, it will end in disgust.

66. 愛極則遷
ài jí zé qiān
When love has reached its highest pitch, it changes its object;

67. 致盈必損
zhì yíng bì sǔn
For whatever has reached fullness must needs decline.

68. 理有固然
lǐ yǒu gù rán
This law is absolute.

69. 美者自美
měi zhě zi měi
The 'beautiful wife who knew herself to be beautiful'

70. 翩以取尤
piān yǐ qǔ yóu
Was soon hated.

71. 冶容求好
yě róng qiú hào
If by a mincing air you seek to please,

72. 君子所讎
jūn zi suǒ chóu
Wise men will abhor you.

73. 結恩而絕
jié ēn ér jué
From this cause truly comes

74. 職此之由
zhí cǐ zhī yóu
The breaking of favour's bond.

The twelve lines make six couplets, and these six further divide in half both according to meaning and rhyme. Lines 63–8 describe the principle by which love is said to grow to fullness and then move on, i.e. that the emperor must call upon all the women of his harem according to a rota, and not be monopolized by one. Most of the lines in this half rhyme (in modern Chinese) with the sound –*an*. The opening lines (63–4), both five characters long, repeat the middle three characters, *bu ke yi* (cannot). In the second half of the passage, lines 69–74, the poet illustrates the principle outlined in the first half with the hypothetical story of the beauty who knew her own beauty, and who painted her face for personal gain. The second halves of the couplets rhyme with the sound –*ou*.

The poem is inscribed on the scroll conventionally in one continuous passage without breaks, reading vertically and from right to left. By only starting a new line when the bottom of the scroll was reached, the passage stretched to three columns and three characters. The reader was expected to work out where the breaks came in the poem, assuming she did not already know it. Each character was written within an imaginary square or rectangle, which was predetermined by its shape. Characters that are naturally tall are somewhat attenuated in upright rectangles; some are naturally square; others are squat and are placed in rectangles that are wider than they are tall.

Because of this deference to the individual qualities of each character, the inscription is not placed in an imaginary square grid, as in more official, public writing. In fact, some of the long, final strokes of the characters (final strokes usually end up in the bottom right corner) 'trespass' outside their designated space. This 'natural' quality in writing was associated with the Wang tradition. An example is the wave-like stroke which in early writings about calligraphy was said to 'rumble' on and on like a peal of thunder, reaching a crescendo and then fading away (*shi* – line 3/character 15, *zhi* – 4/2).

In the Six Dynasties, all the various strokes, from dots to horizontal lines, hooks, flicks and curves, were envisaged as powerful naturalistic images. A dot was said to be like a giant boulder suspended, about to come crashing down to earth from a great height. A vertical stroke was like a dangling withered vine. A downward stroke to the left ending in a sharp point evoked a rhinoceros thrusting its horn into the ground in anger. The long ending stroke extending downwards to the right was like pealing thunder or a breaker crashing to shore. With the smallest of marks, in other words, the calligrapher could not just 'paint' three-dimensional objects, but also harness primal forces, momentum and kinetic energy unleashed in nature. Critics conjured up these images because they regarded the human world as being correlated to nature and the cosmos. Depending on whether or not the human world was in harmony with the cosmos, Heaven meted out punishments and rewards according to the quality of government and leadership. Immoral government brought ecological disaster such as drought, pestilence and flood, as well as civil unrest, whereas just administration brought timely rains, bumper harvests, bounty and prosperity to all. Evoking forms, images and patterns of nature, calligraphy could mediate, almost magically, between sides of this 'correlative universe'.

Over time, the angles and widths of certain strokes, as well as the relationship between elements within characters and their overall proportion has constantly changed. People see writing differently according to what has gone before them and what they wish to achieve with calligraphy. What is so remarkable about Chinese calligraphy is how much new meaning has been created in each era by relatively little apparent change. One of the ways this has been achieved, after the initial development of a fully mature written language in the early Tang dynasty, was by reviving old or ancient styles. Past styles were usually linked in the historical imagination with a certain individual, era or dynasty, whose values and history were well known. A calligrapher could thus express sympathy or longing for a certain style of government or cultural type by actually bringing that time and its aura into the present with modern ancient-style calligraphy. Allusion to the past was a standard way to express one's views in pre-modern times. As time passed, the repertoire of possibilities became so complex that at certain key points in history the canon of calligraphy had to be suddenly simplified, and a new 'synthesis' created. Two of these pivotal moments are the early Yuan dynasty (1271–1368) and the late Ming dynasty (1368–1644). Each is associated with one individual, Zhao Mengfu (1254–1322) and Dong Qichang (1555–1636) respectively, both of whom will reappear in the next chapter.

The calligraphy of the *Admonitions* can, therefore, be placed within a history of the development of Chinese writing style, whether it is a new development in its own right or an ancient style that has been revived in a later period, but still bears the hallmarks of that later period. Comparing it with securely dated examples – we take three examples below – places it in the later Six Dynasties period. In each of these cases, it is not the meaning of the characters that matters, but the similarity in the way they are executed.

The first example is the grave inscription of a noble lady called Meng Jingxun, which dates to 514 and is an example of the style of calligraphy in use in northern China at the end of the Northern Wei dynasty (fig. 50; also see fig. 51). Northern calligraphy of this kind, hewn into stone and set up as part of a monument, is often called 'heroic' in style in contrast to the more intimate southern tradition of 'episto-lary' calligraphy (so-called because of collectors' penchant for calligraphy in letters and hastily scribbled notes). In the Meng Jingxun epitaph, as in the 'rejection' scene inscription, the script is basically standard or 'block' script (*kaishu*), with occasional flourishes of the slightly more cursive 'running' script (*xingshu*). In addition, some unusual forms of characters in the *Admonitions* are also found in the tomb inscription, which places the two fairly close together in date.

A second example is the tomb inscription of Prince Xiao Dan of the Liang dynasty (502–56) in south China, which dates to after 522 (fig. 52; also see fig. 51). Although this tomb inscription (and the Meng Jingxun one) is written in formal block script and is rigidly ordered by a grid, which was customary for calligraphy on monu-ments, some of the characters have the slightly more relaxed feel of 'running' script, as in the *Admonitions*.

A third comparison is with calligraphy believed to be by a southern Buddhist monk called Zhiyong, whose period of activity spanned the Chen (557–89) and Sui (581–617) dynasties. Entitled *Thousand Character Essay* – it is literally a series of one thousand model characters – the Zhiyong text is a manuscript (fig. 53; also see fig. 51), which makes it appear closest of all to the *Admonitions* inscription. Characters written with a brush appear far more fluent than those engraved in stone, and the movement of the brush tip within strokes and the tiny ligatures at the beginning and end of strokes are much clearer. Zhiyong's writing and the *Admonitions* calligraphy have much in common. Look for example at the almost identical and somewhat unusual form of the character *suo*.

Calligraphy dating to before these three examples tends to be squat in form, and to emphasize rectangular horizontal strokes and the flat wave-like stroke, features of Han-dynasty 'clerical' script. In calligraphy of the early Tang dynasty, on the other hand, the strokes are rounded and supple, and the characters are square and perfectly

50 ■ *Epitaph of Meng Jingxun*. Ink rubbing of a stone engraving. Northern Wei dynasty, 514. Palace Museum, Beijing.

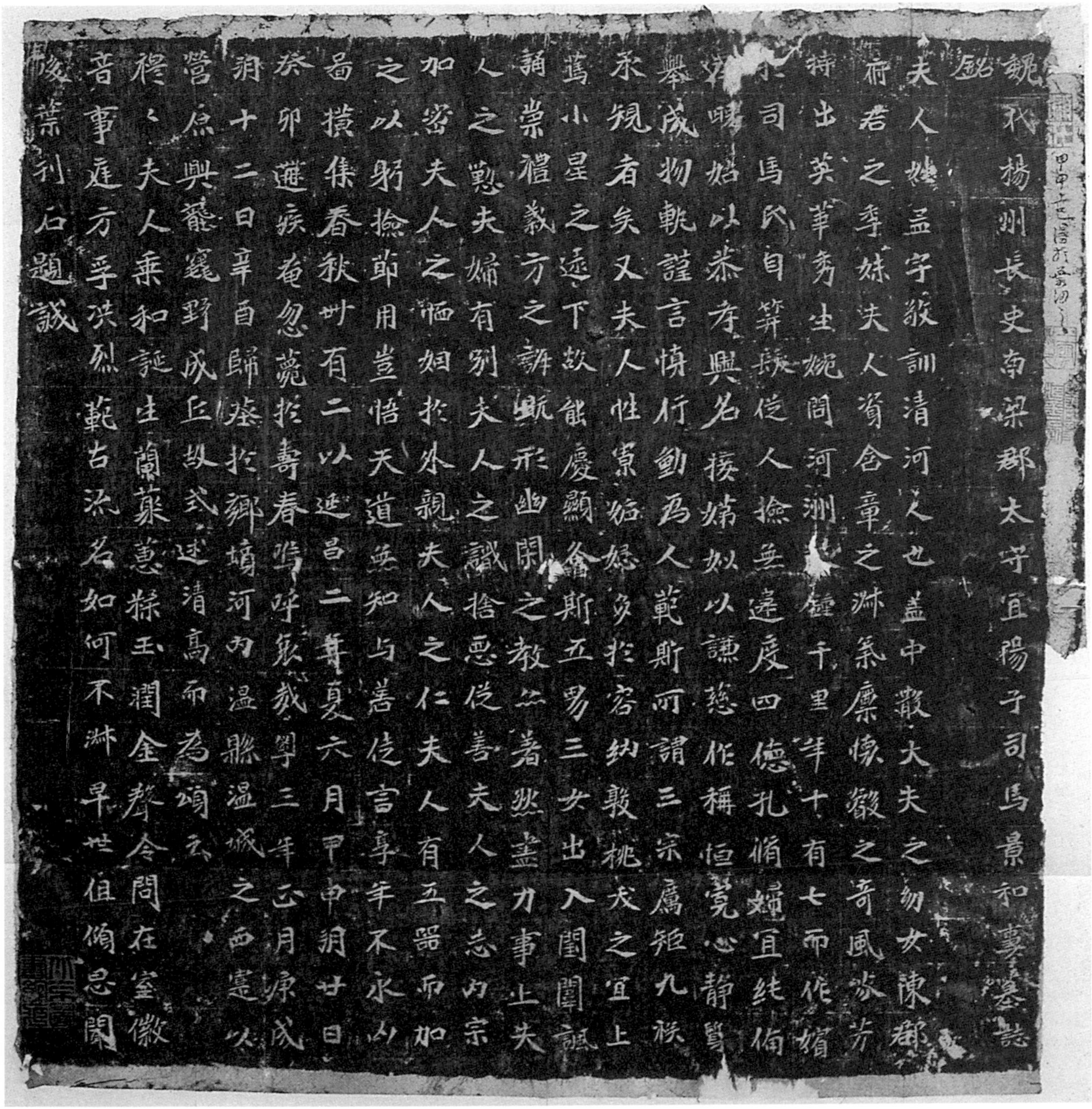

魏揚州長史南梁郡太守宜陽子司馬景和妻孟墓誌

夫人諱敬訓字清河王也蓋中散大夫之少女陳郡
若君之季妹夫人資含章氣稟麗淥懷徽之奇風冰芳
府司馬氏自河洲鐘千里羊有七而作媚
持出英革秀生婉問河洲德以恭箏娥從人捔舉德孔悄嬋宜純俻
曙姑以恭箏娥興名援娣如以謙慈作稱恒覓心靜俻
承成物軏謹言行興好為人戴斯所謂三宗屬殂九祿
舉規者矢又夫人性慷愾始忽多柠容纫毅桃犬之宜九祿
誦之崇禮義方之辭故能景顯魚斯五易三女出入閨闈誠上
鸞小星之懃夫婦有別夫甄形幽開之敎僫善夫人有力之志內宗
人之栅用豈悟天道莫知與善信言享年五器而加
加以密夫人之仔捨惡仗善言享年不永以
之以躬撿節用豈悟天道莫知與善信言享年五
晉摸集香秋冊有二以延昌二年夏六月甲申翔廿日
茶卯進疾奄忽薨於壽莚驊呼哀哉學三年正月廿成
羽十二日辛百歸葬於鄉墳河內溫脇溫城之西窆次
管點興藜襄野成丘述清高而為頌云
後八夫人乘和誃生蘭藜蕙粱玉潤全聳令問在室徽
珍事庭方孚洪烈範古泒名如何不淪旱世徂俻思闈
後葉刊石題誡
音

甲申二七唐於蔡河八

	Admonitions, rejection scene	Meng Jingxun epitaph (514)	Xiao Dan epitaph (after 522)	Zhiyong's *Essay* (latter half 6th century)
bu	不			不
	不			
zhi	之	之 之		之
suo	所			所
hao/xing	好	姓		好
ze	則			則
ci	此			此
ai	愛		隘	愛
shi	寔		是	
en	恩		恩	
zi	子	字	弑	
chou/zhou/jiu	沈	軏	九	
you	由		由	
mei/ren	美	人	臾	美
	美	人	又	
yi	以	以		
ze	目	自		

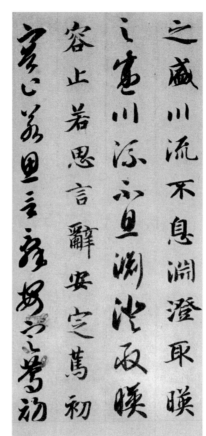

52 ■ Far left: *Epitaph of Xiao Dan.* Liang dynasty (502–56), datable to after 522.

53 ■ Left: Zhiyong (later 6th century). *Thousand Character Essay.* Detail of an album. Ogawa Collection.

balanced, with the left and right and/or upper and lower parts integrated into a composite whole. The calligraphy of the *Admonitions* scroll, which has some of the ancient stiffness but also some of the modern fluency to it, seems to fit most comfortably between these two stages of historical change. There is no suggestion the calligrapher had any knowledge of these later effects, which we would expect had it been copied in the Tang or later. As it does not approximate to the hand of any known calligrapher, we can only attribute it to an unknown hand, probably a court scribe. Also, if we take into account that the *Admonitions* is also a handscroll, it is more likely to have been done at a southern court where this type of mounting was common, rather than in the north, where, from what we now know, stone monuments were more the norm.

4 | Gu Kaizhi and the *Admonitions* in history

We commonly refer to the *Admonitions of the Instructress to the Court Ladies* attributed to Gu Kaizhi as a scroll – the *Admonitions* scroll – but it is not a scroll at all. It has not been a scroll since, for reasons of conservation, it was mounted on two long stretchers, one for the painting and one for everything else in the former scroll, in the period of the First World War (see fig. 73). Its past life – or lives – as a handscroll still partly determines the way we experience the present object: it is still read from right to left. This also creates specific problems when we want to reproduce it in modern book form. But it is important to recognize how at the same time as it shows us the past, its form also shapes our view of that past. We may still imagine viewing it, for instance, as if we were sitting down at a table in a place conducive to reflection, opening it, scrolling through a few feet at a time, and rolling the scroll back at the end. But in its museum case, we view it in the standing, forward-facing posture in which a European picture is gazed at upon a wall, as if through a window frame. So, as neither a scroll for unrolling nor a framed picture on a gallery wall, the *Admonitions* is in fact an intriguing cross between the two, a hybrid of its past and present.

Exemplary of artworks that have come down to us in the East Asian tradition of scroll-mounting, it carries with it an account of its own life in seal impressions, inscriptions penned in fine calligraphy, inventory legends, and so on. These were either placed in the scroll or on the painting by the collectors and connoisseurs through whose hands the artwork passed. As a scroll, it has also been remounted many times, as surviving vestiges of these mountings attest (fig. 54). Thinking about the *Admonitions* as a scroll calls attention to these changes, to ownership, and to what it meant to own it, or even to have viewed it. It clearly meant different things to emperors and to elite collectors and connoisseurs over time. For the former, simply owning it, possessing the past, could confer political legitimacy; for the latter, owning it could be a way to define

54 ■ Silk tapestry, *kesi*, depicting a peony among hydrangeas. A protective outer-wrapper preserved from a Song (960–1279) mounting of the *Admonitions* scroll. The British Museum. These *kesi* tapestries, a new luxury art of 12th-century China, were used to make wrappers of precious scrolls.

one's personal world in one of the few areas of life supposedly free from official or social interference. To refer to the *Admonitions* as a scroll is, then, to recognize how this aspect of its history has contributed to its position as a monumental work of art.

On one hand, the legacy of the handscroll opens up refreshing and unique views into past history of a kind that might not exist in other cultures. On the other, this wealth of material, circumscribing the artwork like a frame placed around it, compels us to approach the artwork through this frame, to consider the painting in light of this particular history, and to exclude other possibilities and interpretations. In this respect, the scroll mounting that perhaps still most powerfully shapes our mental image of the *Admonitions* is that of the Qianlong emperor of the Qing dynasty, who acquired it for the imperial collection and had it remounted in about 1746. For this man, the scroll was a 'divine omen of antiquity' that had appeared in the world to legitimate him and his political ideology. But the point of art history, and in particular social art history, is to investigate not just the representation of the emperor's – or whoever's – power, but also the power of representation. How have the various forms of the scroll encouraged unique ways of understanding the painting?

The *Admonitions* scroll tells the story of an extraordinary journey through history. The idea in these pages has been to put the work of art first, before history, insofar as it is itself prime evidence for history. It would be rash to allow history to explain it when it is in itself an authoritative source of that history. By visualizing its story this way and by focusing on what its many owners did to it (remounting it, impressing seals, and so on) and thought of it (and wrote down in books), we may try to interpret these changes historically. Where certain additions to the scroll are recognized as being later than they purport to be, we should not simply dismiss them as 'fake'. Instead, we may try to explain what called for them. For instance, we should recognize that early paintings did not have signatures, but at some point in time collectors began to see this as an omission that had to be put right, first with an attribution and later with the insertion of a 'fake' signature. We can use one artwork – albeit a very important one – to begin just such a history of art, collecting and connoisseurship, and we are justified in doing this because the object of art is itself a piece of history. This study of the *Admonitions* scroll's provenance through the world of art and collecting, therefore, considers stages in its history according to ownership and mounting.

To 1127

The earliest written record of the *Admonitions* scroll is in a book entitled *History of Painting*, completed in 1103, by Mi Fu (1052–1107), a pre-eminent but notorious calligrapher, painter, connoisseur and collector of the late Northern Song period. According to Mi Fu, in the late eleventh century the painting was in the keeping of a senior palace eunuch, Liu Youfang, who served the imperial family through the reigns of several Song emperors, including Shenzong (r. 1068–85) and Zhezong (r. 1086–1100). The *Admonitions* then resurfaces shortly afterwards in the *Xuanhe Painting Manual*, the catalogue of the imperial painting collection of the late Northern Song emperor and artist, Huizong (r. 1101–25), completed in 1120, but there appear to be no other written records until the Ming period.

Mi Fu's association of the painting with Gu Kaizhi is somewhat tentative, and it is unclear whether this was his own personal attribution or a generally accepted view. In the Song emperor Huizong's catalogue, however, the painting is among nine listed under the heading 'Gu Kaizhi', meaning that it was now authenticated as a genuine work by Gu Kaizhi. This was a most privileged position, because 'Gu Kaizhi' was the first artist to be listed in the prime category, 'Buddhist and Daoist Subjects' (i.e. religious figure paintings). For emperor Huizong, the Confucian subject matter was evidently of secondary interest compared to Gu Kaizhi's reputation as a peerless talent whose works were marvels of skill and profound subtlety.

As well as having the scrolls in his collection carefully documented, Huizong had them lavishly mounted with silk and damask end-panels. He reserved the use of precious silk *kesi* tapestries depicting auspicious flowers, dragons and buildings, a new luxury art of the early twelfth century, for making the outer wrappers of scrolls. The silk tapestry depicting a peony among hydrangeas (fig. 54) and silk brocade end-panels (fig. 67) that are features of the *Admonitions* scroll today could well have been part of the mounting that Huizong had made for it. The peony conjures up ideas of wealth and honour (*fugui*, a pun on the Chinese word for peony), but was also a poetic and mildly erotic image of female beauty. The transcription of the last few admonitions in 'slender-gold' script (fig. 56), a style of calligraphy Huizong pioneered, was believed to be by his hand until recently, when it was reattributed to his great-grandson, the Jin emperor Zhangzong, to whom we turn presently.

Seals are rarely reliable evidence in their own right for dating a work of art, and the *Admonitions* scroll exemplifies this. Ming and later connoisseurs have had a penchant for fabricating histories for works of art by impressing spurious early seals on them. Seals on the *Admonitions* painting and end-panels that purport to be of the Emperor Huizong are thought to be just such forgeries, because they are poorly carved and their placement does not conform to the standard protocol he used, which has been meticulously reconstructed by modern scholars. The seal that purports to be the earliest is one of the Office for the Dissemination of Culture (Hongwenguan), a government department of the early Tang dynasty (618–907). Its dissimilarity to other impressions and its curious placement beside the 'signature' of Gu Kaizhi at the end of the painting betray it as a spurious later addition, perhaps of the late Ming dynasty, when the appearance of such an 'ancient' seal would have greatly appealed to the imagination of collectors and aesthetes.

There is, however, one early seal impressed on the *Admonitions* painting, which is widely accepted as genuine. It is a very large imperial seal with the legend 'Sagacious Contemplation, East Wing' (Ruisi Dongge), which is an abbreviation for the East Wing of the Palace of Sagacious Contemplation, part of a building in the Northern Song imperial palace city. Records indicate that this palace was built late in the reign of the emperor Shenzong in 1075, so it is accepted that the *Admonitions* painting predates this time. The seal was originally impressed at the top in each scene, although some stamps have faded or had other seals impressed on top of them (see e.g. figs 20, 33). Its size and the 'lofty' calligraphy of its legend lend this imperial seal great dignity, and put its authenticity beyond doubt. This particular palace is not known for having been a storehouse of imperial art treasures – it was in fact a venue for imperial audiences and state events, such as banquets. Its name, 'Sagacious Contemplation', implies it was a place the emperor used for private activities and study. Certainly we know that Emperor Huizong housed there perhaps the greatest calligraphic treasure of the Northern Song period – a stone stele engraved in the Tang dynasty with the *Orchid Pavilion Preface* originally written by the Calligraphic Sage Wang Xizhi, a near contemporary of Gu Kaizhi (fig. 55). It would have made a tidy parallel to have masterpieces by Wang Xizhi and Gu Kaizhi housed – and perhaps from time to time exhibited together – separately from the remainder of the imperial collection, though whether this was the case is speculative.

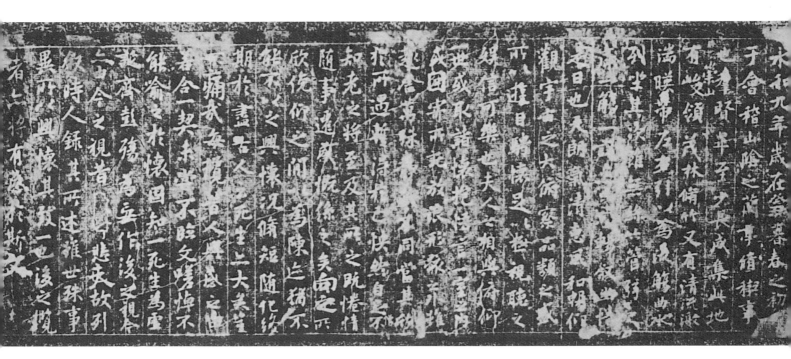

The fact that the eunuch Liu Youfang had the painting in his possession tells us that it moved between different precincts of the imperial city in the second half of the Northern Song, and passed through the hands of senior palace staff as well as emperors and – presumably – their wives. It thus served different functions. In Emperor Shenzong's Palace of Sagacious Contemplation, it was perhaps an aid to self-study. In the hands of Liu Youfang, it may have reverted to being a tool of admonition. In the course of a distinguished career, Liu Youfang's responsibilities included presenting congratulations, and no doubt gifts, to members of the imperial family on the emperor's behalf. On occasion, he may also have had to issue reprimands to wayward palace women, and therefore could have been instructed to use the *Admonitions* as an object of warning. Later, as Emperor Huizong amassed a collection of art, the *Admonitions* came to be regarded as a supreme work of realism, and may even have been used to teach Academy painters specializing in 'Buddhist and Daoist subjects' and 'figures'.

55 ■ Wang Xizhi (303–61). *Orchid Pavilion Preface.* Ink rubbing made from an engraving of the calligraphy in stone. Song dynasty (960–1279). These rubbings are now usually mounted in handscrolls.

1127–1276

Huizong was a great aesthete, but he was an ineffectual ruler, and eventually lost his capital and north China in 1126–7 to the invading Jurchens, who had founded their Jin or Golden dynasty in 1115. So began a century and a half of political division, with south China remaining under the Southern Song dynasty, and north China initially under the Jurchen Jin. The thirteenth century saw the arrival of the Mongols, who crushed the Jin in 1234 and the Southern Song in 1276 to reunify the country and incorporate it into their vast empire. Tracing the provenance of the *Admonitions* through these turbulent years has not proved easy, in part because of the bias in later history in favour of the native Southern Song dynasty, which was deemed to have inherited the 'mandate of Heaven', the mantle of the legitimate ruler of China.

In 1126–7, Huizong and many members of the Song imperial family were captured and held hostage by the Jin. Some of the court did escape south, including one of Huizong's sons who would become emperor Gaozong (r. 1127–62) of the Southern Song dynasty. Huizong died in captivity, but not before he had married many of his daughters to Jurchen princes, rivals to Huizong's descendants in the ruling house of the Southern Song. We know that following the fall of the Northern Song capital Bianliang (modern Kaifeng, Henan Province) in 1126–7, the Jurchens took possession of Huizong's imperial collection after its whereabouts was betrayed to them by a eunuch. We would assume the *Admonitions* scroll now passed from Huizong's collection to the Jurchen. There are, however, some possible flaws in this argument.

One is the presence of seals on the *Admonitions* that may have belonged to palace women of the Southern Song dynasty. If genuine, they would suggest these women used the scroll to cultivate the moral lessons described in it. If spurious, they probably represent a later collector's preference for the idea that the scroll went south with the Song, and did not end up in Jurchen hands. To have fabricated a provenance through the Southern Song harem, however, was perhaps to 'gild the lily'.

Another difficulty with the Northern Song to Jin provenance is the existence of the ink-outline copy of the *Admonitions*, now in the Palace Museum in Beijing. On the basis of style as well as the appearance of 'taboo' characters (i.e. emperors' personal names) in the inscriptions, it is thought to have been copied from the 'original' – the British Museum scroll – at the court of the Southern Song emperor Xiaozong

(r. 1163–89). One of the end-panels of the British Museum scroll bears seals of Jin emperor Zhangzong (r. 1189–1208), Huizong's great-grandson, but it seems likely these were not incorporated into the scroll until a later date. Possibly the Beijing copy was made as a record of an original that was to be presented to the Jurchens as a diplomatic gift. However, given the acrimonious relations between the Southern Song and the Jin, it seems unlikely that such a work of art as the *Admonitions* scroll would have passed back and forth lightly between the two regimes.

The Jin emperor Zhangzong admired his great-grandfather Huizong, and closely modelled his calligraphy on Huizong's. Named after the taut, narrow strokes and 'precious' use of ink, the 'slender-gold' calligraphy of the two emperors is very alike. Jin Zhangzong did not sign his writings, and it is only recently that individual traits in some of his characters have enabled scholars to distinguish his calligraphy from Huizong's. In part because of the anti-Jin bias of historians, all 'slender-gold' calligraphy used to be ascribed to Huizong, including the transcription of the last few 'admonitions' from Zhang Hua's poem on brown silk that is now part of the scroll (fig. 56). Today, however, this inscription is attributed to Jin Zhangzong.

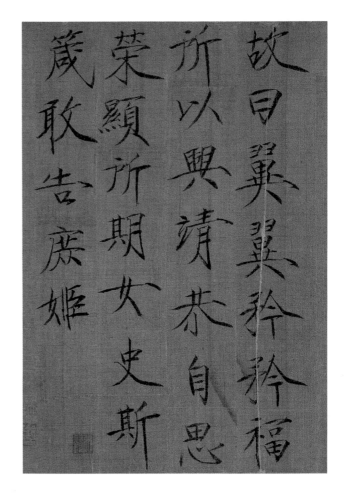

56 ■ Transcription of the last two admonitions in 'slender-gold' script, formerly mounted as a colophon in the *Admonitions* scroll. Attributed to Jin emperor Zhangzong (r. 1189–1208); traditionally attributed to Song emperor Huizong (r. 1101–25).

As noted above, this inscription was probably not mounted in the *Admonitions* scroll at this time, but was part of another scroll. The inventory of the collection of the disgraced sixteenth-century minister Yan Song, to which we come below, refers to an *Admonitions* painting and a transcription of the text in 'slender-gold' script calligraphy as two different scrolls, and they were probably not mounted together for the first time until shortly after that. Zhangzong's inscription was originally written on a higher length of silk than the one the painting is on, and had to be cut up and reassembled in shorter columns so as to fit into the *Admonitions* scroll, as new ultraviolet photography

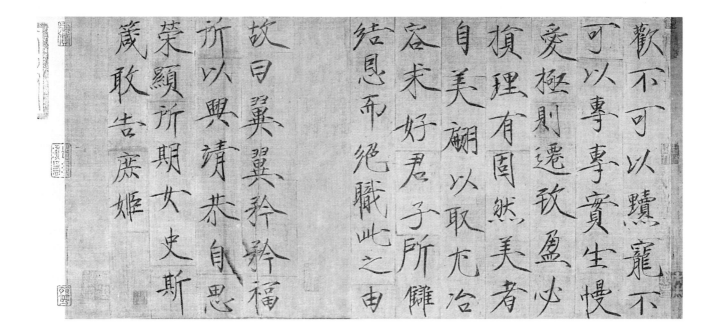

57 ■ The 'slender gold' inscription photographed under ultraviolet light. The cuts in the silk illustrate how the inscription was carved up and reassembled, so as to fit inside the *Admonitions* scroll, probably in the late Ming period (1368–1644).

has dramatically confirmed (fig. 57). At least we can say that this inscription was not written to accompany this painting.

The provenance of the scroll in the thirteenth century is no less convoluted. If it was in Jin Zhangzong's collection, we would assume that it came into the Mongol imperial collection when the Mongols overran the Jin in 1234. However, by the third quarter of the thirteenth century, the *Admonitions* scroll was in the hands of the Southern Song chief minister Jia Sidao (1213–75), as two prominent seals of his at the bottom of one of the end-panels attest. Jia Sidao wielded immense power at the Southern Song court, but is reviled in Chinese history for having betrayed the Song dynasty to the Mongols. An insatiable art collector as well as a political double-dealer, Jia Sidao had extensive contacts in Mongol-occupied north China, including spies and agents who acquired works of art for him. Although he could have obtained the *Admonitions* scroll through them, it is also possible that it was a gift or bribe from a Mongol prince or khan, perhaps even the great Khubilai Khan (r. 1260–94). Unfortunately, the *Admonitions* does not appear on a surviving inventory of major works in Jia Sidao's collection. When he was eventually disgraced and cashiered shortly before the collapse of the dynasty, his art collection should have become state property and gone into the Southern Song imperial collection. Not long after, in 1276, Khubilai overran the corrupt and crumbling Southern Song and reunified China. Officials in the Mongol government now took possession of the former Southern Song imperial collection in Hangzhou. A connoisseur called Wang Yun (1227–1304) was charged with inventory-ing and sending the best pieces to the Yuan capital at Beijing. The *Admonitions* does not appear on his list, suggesting it was already in private hands.

1276–1562

We cannot be certain who owned the *Admonitions* in the Yuan and early to middle Ming dynasties. Indeed, during the Yuan dynasty, the scroll seems to have 'gone to ground', for it is not listed in the writings, inventories or catalogues of any of the prominent art connoisseurs, such as Zhou Mi (1232–98), Zhao Mengfu and Tang Hou (act. mid-1250s–1310s), who were most likely to have seen it. It was still an important painting subject, and its composition was known from an ink-outline copy by Li Gonglin recorded by Zhou Mi. This may have been the Beijing copy, or another similar painting. Returning to the British Museum scroll, a seal reading 'Ali' may belong to a Uighur official called Ali who served in south China in the late thirteenth century and owned a small collection of works of Chinese calligraphy. Another seal on the scroll has been tentatively identified as belonging to a fourteenth-century Chan Buddhist monk. A short inscription giving an official-looking inventory serial number, reading 'Scrolls category, number X', on the front border-panel could have been added at any date between the Yuan and the late Ming. A seal linked with the distinguished Grand Secretary to the Ming Zhengde emperor (r. 1506–21), Wang Ao (1450–1524), suggests the scroll was in his collection in the fifteenth century. Some time between 1542–62, the scroll came into the hands of the powerful but corrupt Grand Secretary, Yan Song (1480–1565). After Yan was toppled in a palace coup of 1562, his vast col-lection was confiscated by the government, and inventoried in 1569 by the scholar-painter Wen Jia (1501–83), a member of the prominent Wen family of Suzhou.

The Yuan dynasty is a pivotal moment in Chinese art history, on account of the reformation of the visual arts engineered by the Chinese-educated elite under Mongol rule. Tracing perceptions of and attitudes toward Gu Kaizhi provides insight into the

58 ■ Zhao Mengfu
(1254–1322). *Mind Landscape
of Xie Youyu*, early 1290s.
Detail of a handscroll; ink and
colour on silk, 27.4 × 117.0 cm.
Princeton University Art
Museum. Museum Purchase,
Fowler McCormick, Class of
1921, Fund (1984–13).

process, which opened the way for later 'literati painting' in China. Let us take the
example of how a lost portrait by Gu Kaizhi of a politician he admired called Xie Kun
(or Xie Youyu; 280–322), who lived about a century before him at the beginning of
the Eastern Jin, was reinvented. Gu's portrait was recreated in the early 1290s at the
court of Khubilai Khan by the leading Chinese scholar-official painter of the early
Yuan dynasty, Zhao Mengfu (1254–1322). In this painting, the *Mind Landscape of Xie*

Youyu, Zhao Mengfu conjured up the archaic style he imagined Gu had used (fig. 58). The solitary figure of the politician sits on a tiger skin at the entrance to a cave in a hill by a stream lined with pines and magnolias. Gu Kaizhi's biographies tell how he was asked why he had painted his subject in this setting, and Gu replied that Xie Kun had described himself as having excelled in 'hill and dale', meaning that even as an urbane courtier, Xie Kun had cherished and maintained the free-spirited mentality of the rustic – he was what was known as a 'recluse at court'. 'Thus it is quite appropriate that he be depicted in hill and dale,' Gu remarked.

Seeking to describe ambivalence about his controversial decision as a Chinese aristocrat to serve at the Mongol court, the young Zhao Mengfu reinvented Gu Kaizhi's formula in the *Mind Landscape*, giving pictorial form to the idea that he was himself a 'recluse at court'. Consciously primitive effects, such as the simple, calligraphic rock outlines, the archaistic spatial handling of the cave, the emblematic shapes of the trees, as well as the authentic lack of a signature (for early paintings cannot have had artist's signatures), are used to create the painting. The tree shapes and rock outlines have parallels in calligraphy, the artistic mode through which Zhao Mengfu interpreted Gu Kaizhi. He would have learned Gu's linear technique, known as 'lofty, ancient, gossamer-line', and other stylistic features from extant works that he was able to see in imperial, official and private collections. We cannot be certain he saw the *Admonitions*, but he must have known early paintings of similar quality, including some of the *Goddess of the Luo River* scrolls, which were then believed to be by Gu Kaizhi. For Zhao Mengfu, Gu Kaizhi represented the beginning of Chinese painting. Crucially, what he learned from this visit back to the origins of the tradition shaped subsequent returns to old masters spanning the period between Gu Kaizhi and himself throughout his career, as he worked out a comprehensive critical reassessment of China's artistic heritage.

Zhao Mengfu did not leave a book of his thoughts on art, but many of his views are found in the writings of his contemporary, Tang Hou. Tang Hou's *Mirror of Painting* mentions several paintings by Gu Kaizhi that he had seen, including a version of the *Goddess of the Luo River* (though it is not clear which one). Tang Hou's entry on Gu Kaizhi made a major contribution to art-historical thinking, for he conjured up an image, destined to be much repeated by later critics, of Gu's gossamer-like, delicate and thin lineament. This was his image of the 'spring silkworm spitting silk threads'. As China was now subjugated into the vast Eurasian empire of the Mongols, men like

59 ■ Wei Jiuding (14th century). *Goddess of the Luo River*, with inscription by Ni Zan (1301–74), dated 1368. Detail of a hanging scroll; ink on paper, 90.8 × 31.8 cm. National Palace Museum, Taipei.

Tang Hou aspired to a measure of cultural if not political autonomy. This concept brilliantly highlighted the sophistication and richness of the Chinese cultural heritage both nationally and internationally, for China had long been revered across the continent as the land of silk.

From the late Yuan and into the Ming period, figure painting lost critical ground to landscape painting and calligraphy, which now occupied the minds of literati artists and critics, and many court and professional artists. Gu Kaizhi remained the founding figure in the evolving painting tradition: he was still called the 'ancestor of painting' by the leading early Ming calligrapher Shen Du (1357–1434). We illustrate two important exceptions to the general trend towards landscape. One is the *Goddess of the Luo River* (fig. 59), which shows a Gu Kaizhi-style figure, her drapery and scarves billowing out in the wind, in a typically fourteenth-century landscape setting. An inscription of 1368 by the landscape master Ni Zan (1301–74) attributes the painting of this 'modest, retiring beauty' (*yaotiao*) to the little-known Wei Jiuding. A second exception is an early work by the Suzhou master, Wen Zhengming (1470–1559), entitled *Goddess and Lady of the Xiang River* (fig. 60), a lyrical work painted in subtle colour washes and a pale ink outline. In this picture, the beauty holding a fan fixes her eyes upon her companion behind her, who looks ahead stoically, rather in the way that Lady Ban does in the *Admonitions*. The waisted forms of their bodies recall figures in the *Benevolent and Wise Women* painting attributed to Gu Kaizhi, as well as those in the *Admonitions*. In the inscription to his painting, Wen Zhengming says that on the instructions of his teacher he copied a work of the same title by Zhao Mengfu, and that he had tried to capture the sense of the ancient model that Zhao had in his painting. This conveys not only how important Gu Kaizhi was to these later masters, but also how influential Zhao Mengfu's creative methodology of learning from old master pictures was in later painting.

1562–1746

Between the late Ming and the Qianlong emperor's acquisition of the scroll, the *Admonitions* passed through the hands and before the eyes of quite a number of leading connoisseurs and artists. The year 1562 marked the start of a period of frequent changes of ownership. Having been acquired by Yan Song, probably during his twenty-year stint as Grand Secretary under the Jiajing emperor (1622–66), the scroll was confiscated by the government after he was toppled in a palace coup of that year. The painting is mentioned – as being by 'a Jin artist', not by Gu Kaizhi – in the inventory of Yan Song's property made by Wen Jia, Wen Zhengming's son. Wen Jia also records a scroll of 'Admonitions' calligraphy in 'slender-gold' script that he believed to be by Song emperor Huizong. This is likely to have been the transcription of the last few

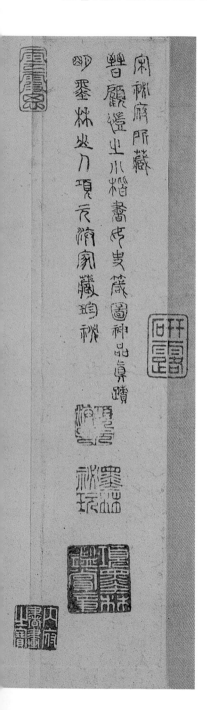

admonitions which is now part of the 'colophons panel'; the painting and 'slender-gold' inscription were probably mounted together in the same scroll shortly after.

In the decades after 1562, many major scrolls changed hands frequently. In these times of financial crisis and political instability, the late Ming emperors occasionally resorted to paying their senior ministers with artworks in kind. When large collections like Yan Song's were confiscated by the government, the contents could be sold off cheaply to imperial princes, or they ended up in the collections of the most powerful ministers. At different stages, corrupt palace eunuchs had opportunity to sell off official or confiscated property illicitly, probably with the collusion of emperors. It is possible the *Admonitions* got its official-looking 'half' inventory number when it was impounded by the government around this time.

By about the 1560s, the scroll had entered the collection of the much-respected connoisseur and scholar-official Gu Congyi (1523–88), where it was seen by a fellow connoisseur He Liangjun (1506–73). He Liangjun described it as being 'by Gu Kaizhi, and having only figures [... which have] a lifelike spirit, seemingly wanting to walk'. Not long afterwards, the *Admonitions* scroll was acquired by the tycoon pawnbroker Xiang Yuanbian (1525–90), owner of the largest and finest art collection in the late Ming. An inveterate stamper of his seals, Xiang Yuanbian tattooed the scroll and the painting itself – which up to now had been relatively unencumbered by seals – with some fifty seal impressions. Connoisseurs and critics at this time expected that a work of art, and especially one so prized as the *Admonitions*, should become the cause of an obsession on the part of its owner. They even criticised collectors who failed to be sufficiently obsessed. But they also recognized how an antique artefact could create a personally-defined ideal realm over which its owner alone could 'roam', in principle free from social or official regulation. To judge by his colophon and the archaic script he chose to execute it in, Xiang Yuanbian deeply treasured the scroll's antiquity and its imperial provenance (fig. 61):

A treasure of the Song imperial palace.

The *Admonitions of the Court Instructress* picture and calligraphy in small block script by Gu Kaizhi of the Jin; divine category, genuine traces.

Treasured possession of the family of Xiang Yuanbian, Ink Forest Mountain Man ['pen name'], of the Ming.

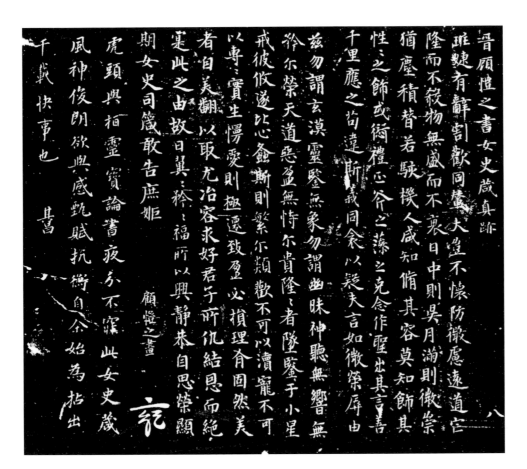

千載快事也　甚昌

風神俊朗欲與感甄賦抗衡自余始為拈出

虎頭與栢靈寶論書疲分不窮此女史蔵

期女史司箴敢告庶姫　顧愷之畫

莫此之由故曰翼以福所以興靜恭自思榮顯

者自美翻以取尤冶容求好君子所仇結恩而絕

以專之實生慢愛則趣遠致盈必損理有固然美

戒彼依依此心無論則繁爾類歡不可以瀆寵不可

慈勿謂玄漠靈鑒無象勿謂幽昧神聽無響無

矜爾榮天道惡盈無恃爾貴隆鑒于小星

千里應之苟違斯義同衾以疑夫言如微榮辱由

性之飾或衛禮正容作聖出其言善

猶塵積替若駿機人咸知修其容莫知飾其

隆而不殺物無盛而不衰日中則昃月滿則微崇

班婕有辭割歡同輦夫豈不懷防微慮遠道它

晋顧愷之畫女史蔵真跡

顧愷之畫

61 ■ Opposite page: Xiang Yuanbian's (1525–90) colophon to the *Admonitions*.

62 ■ Dong Qichang (1555–1636). Transcription of the *Admonitions* inscriptions, and colophon. Detail from Dong's woodblock printed compendium, *Copybook of the Hall of Playing Geese*, 1603.

It has been suggested that in addition to impressing his own seals, Xiang Yuanbian was the person responsible for impressing the many spurious seals of Song emperors. If they were believed authentic, those old seals would have greatly increased the scroll's value in the art market, but, whether credible or not, they would have made the possibility that the scroll was 'a treasure of the Song imperial palace' more tangible, and hence greatly increased the scroll's interest to an obsessive collector such as Xiang Yuanbian.

At this time the scroll was seen by the towering artist and scholar-official of this era Dong Qichang (1555–1636), who studied Xiang's collection. In a colophon to a

Song landscape painting now in Tokyo National Museum (fig. 65), Dong Qichang singled out the *Admonitions* and three landscape paintings by Li Gonglin as 'four pre-eminent handscrolls' that had belonged to Gu Congyi. On the strength of Gu Congyi and Dong Qichang's interest in them, these four would later become the famous Four Beauties, the most important paintings in the huge collection of the Qianlong emperor. Intriguingly, however, it was not the painting of the *Admonitions* scroll that most impressed Dong Qichang, a calligrapher and landscape painter – it was the calligraphic inscriptions accompanying each illustration. He believed them to be by Gu Kaizhi himself. Dong Qichang devoutly copied and reproduced them at the beginning of his 1603 compendium of ancient models of calligraphy, *Copybook of the Hall of Playing Geese* (the 'playing geese' were the great masters of calligraphy; fig. 62). To accompany them, he wrote a colophon comparing the 'refined spirit' of Gu Kaizhi's 'Admonitions' inscriptions with one of the great works of the calligraphic canon, the transcription of the 'Goddess of the Luo River Ode' by Wang Xianzhi (344–88) (see fig. 49), son of the Calligraphic Sage Wang Xizhi. But he was insistent the 'Admonitions' calligraphy was by Gu Kaizhi. For Dong Qichang and fellow late Ming collectors and connoisseurs, the scroll was valued as a 'talismanic relic' of Eastern Jin calligraphy, and not as a painting.

In 1616, the *Admonitions* scroll is mentioned in the catalogue of a connoisseur called Zhang Chou (1577–1643), who was the first to record the 'signature' of Gu Kaizhi at the end of the painting. This spurious cipher had probably been only recently added, perhaps by its late owner, Xiang Yuanbian. Not long afterwards, the scroll was in the collection of a wealthy southern collector, Zhang Xiaosi (act. *c.* 1640–70), and after that, the collection of a Qing official called Da Zhongguang (1623–92), also a painter and calligrapher. In 1672, it was noted by the connoisseur Zhu Yizun (1629–1709) as having been in the possession of the Wang family of Jiangdu. In the middle of the Kangxi reign (1662–1722), it was in the hands of a senior government minister called Liang Qingbiao (1620–91), the owner of a large collection which also included the monochrome copy of the *Admonitions* and *Benevolent and Wise Women* now in the Palace Museum, Beijing (figs 8, 9).

Another connoisseur of the Kangxi period, Wu Sheng, recorded the scroll in detail in his book *Record of Great Views* of about 1712. This record was again most concerned with the authorship of the calligraphy and remarked that Dong Qichang had

had the 'Admonitions' inscriptions published in his calligraphy copybook to establish for good that they were not by Wang Xianzhi, but by the hand of Gu Kaizhi himself.

At about this time, the scroll was acquired by the family of An Qi (1683–1746?), a wealthy Korean salt merchant, in whose 1742 painting catalogue, *Record of Views of the Ink Garden (Moyuan huiguan lu)*, it is once more described in detail. An Qi's remarks on the contents and details of the scroll indicate how he admired it as a complete article. He talked, for instance, of the delicate ink outlines, which he compared to the 'gossamer threads of spring silkworms'; of Gu Kaizhi's signature and calligraphy; of the

unusual inventory mark in 'half-characters'; of the 'slender-gold' inscription, which he believed had been incorporated into the scroll by Liang Qingbiao; of the *kesi* tapestry outer wrapper and jade toggle. It was, he said, 'truly beautiful to behold!' Along with much of An Qi's collection, the *Admonitions* passed into the hands of the Qianlong emperor shortly after his death.

We have seen above how the late Ming figure painter Ding Yunpeng reworked the scene of Lady Feng and the bear in a handscroll composition. In fact, this painting bore little relation to the art of Gu Kaizhi, although its composition was loosely modelled on the same scene in the *Admonitions*. As we have also noted above, figure painting received scant attention from high-ranking arbiters of literati taste such as Dong Qichang. Despite a lack of critical regard, figure painting, especially portraits and birthday pictures, was now prized by the urban *nouveaux riches*. One of the leading figure painters catering for this market was a most unconventional member of the educated elite called Chen Hongshou (1598–1652).

64 ■ Chen Hongshou (1598–1652) and assistant Yan Zhan. *Portrait of He Tianzhang.* Detail of a handscroll; ink and colour on silk, 25.3 × 163.2 cm. Suzhou Museum.

Frustrated in his attempts to gain the relative financial and social security of a position in the civil service or government, Chen Hongshou became a professional painter, and used bizarre, ancient techniques to disturb his viewers' expectations. He turned to unconventional sources such as ancient figural styles found in stone rubbings preserved in temples, as well as the popular images in prints and pattern-books that uneducated professional painters used. His unusual sources and style represented a clear – one could even say ironic – challenge to the dominant trends in painting, as did his artistic practice, which included work for the highly competitive new industry of woodblock-print-illustrated publishing. Chen Hongshou was among the first artists also recognized as painters to design prints (fig. 63); and (like his European contemporary Rembrandt) he also ran a studio. Although Chen Hongshou's figural style was not directly modelled on Gu Kaizhi's, but on the early figural tradition Gu Kaizhi had begun, his off-beat sense of humour, his portrayals of beauties and his lyrical linear style were all unconventional in his day and do make him seem like a latter-day Gu Kaizhi. In the *Portrait of He Tianzhang*, the beauty's long scalloped shawl is a playful reference to this feature in the painting of Gu Kaizhi (fig. 64).

1746 to the First World War (1914–18)

The period from 1746 to World War I covers the time in which the *Admonitions* painting was mounted in the handscroll created for it, as the most important painting in the imperial collection, by the Manchu emperor of China known as Qianlong (r. 1736–95). A contemporary of imperial rulers including Frederick the Great of Prussia (r. 1740–86), George II of England (r. 1727–60), and Louis XV of France (r. 1715–74), the Qianlong emperor was also their rival. It would be well worth considering what the equivalent of the *Admonitions* scroll might have been in collections of these European monarchs – a treasure like the Bayeux tapestry, perhaps, in the case of Louis XV?

65 ■ Li of Shucheng (12th century). *Xiao and Xiang Rivers*. Traditionally ascribed to Li Gonglin (*c*.1049–1106). Detail of a handscroll; ink on paper, 30.4 × 400.4 cm. Tokyo National Museum.

The emperor Qianlong competed with these rulers to be patron to the greatest men of learning and artists of the day. He also maintained a vice-like grip over his Chinese dominion, and was masterly in his use of learning and the arts to stabilize Manchu rule.

When the Qianlong emperor had the *Admonitions* remounted, we assume he included everything that had been mounted with it previously, but he also made a number of significant changes and additions. These included a new patterned blue-brocade outer protective wrapper (frontispiece) on which he attached a buff label inscribed in his own calligraphy with the legend,

> The 'Admonitions of the Instructress to the Court Ladies' painted by Gu Kaizhi, including his calligraphic inscriptions; genuine traces. A trinket [work of art] of the Inner Palace. Divine Category.

This wrapper matched that placed around the handscroll containing the *Xiao and Xiang Rivers* painting in Tokyo National Museum (fig. 65), which, as we will see below, was part of the same set of four most treasured paintings in his collection.

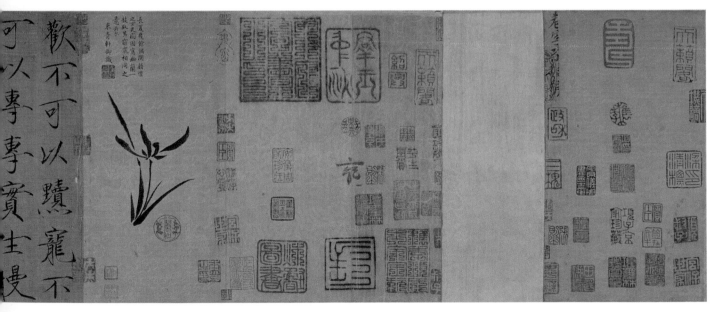

The interior of Qianlong's *Admonitions* may be reassembled as follows (see fig. 73). After the Song tapestry, he first added his title-piece in three very large characters, which reads 'fragrance of the red reed', an allusion to the tool mentioned in the Confucian classics that was used by the instructress to admonish her peers (fig. 66). This emperor evidently wanted the scroll to be understood as a tool for correction, rather than as a free-spirited work of art. A close examination of these characters – confirmed by ultraviolet photography – reveals that they were not written in fluent strokes of a brush, but were outlined, filled in and touched up by the emperor's assistants. The Qianlong emperor also owned the Beijing copy of the *Admonitions*, which he believed to be by Li Gonglin, and he composed a similar title-piece for it. It reads 'the beginning of kingship', a classical allusion to a passage where the budding sage-king finds himself a worthy mate, a chaste, retiring (*yaotiao*) woman of great virtue and beauty (fig. 46).

On the end-panel of patterned yellow silk, the Qianlong emperor added a small painting of an orchid in a dozen strokes of the brush (it has received little praise by modern art historians), below an inscription in small characters reading: 'One summer evening at a moment of leisure, I chanced to view Gu Kaizhi's *Court Instructress* painting, and sketched this single lonely orchid. Both express the idea of the "chaste, retiring beauty". Imperially inscribed in the Arrival of Verdance Pavilion [Laiqingxuan]' (figs 47, 67). The 'chaste, retiring beauty' alluded again to the ideal partner for the ancient sage-king: a stunningly beautiful woman of profound moral refinement, who, if seen at all, is seen from behind as she modestly retires to her own quarters. As the Qianlong emperor viewed the scroll in his private quarters, the *Admonitions* scroll conjured up the image of a woman who had perfected all its lessons – his perfect mate. He pictured her as the fragrant wild orchid, an age-old symbol of loyalty to the ruler.

Intriguingly, this image of a Chinese beauty was no doubt all the more desirable for being unobtainable, at least in theory. The Manchu rulers repeatedly banned intermarriage between Manchus and other races, reputedly to preserve Manchu racial and cultural integrity. Despite this injunction, the Qianlong emperor is said to have heaped favours upon a Muslim beauty from the western regions called Xiangfei, 'Fragrant Concubine', who had betrayed her people to the Qing and whom he made a concubine.

We should not be taken in too easily, therefore, by the Qianlong emperor's devout Confucian rhetoric on the *Admonitions*. While he may genuinely have devoted

66 ■ Opposite page, above: 'Fragrance of a red reed', title-piece to the *Admonitions* scroll by the Qianlong emperor, datable to *c.* 1746. Ultraviolet photography shows these three characters, *tong guan fang*, to have been outlined and filled in with ink: they may have been executed by mounters replicating an imperial inscription.

67 ■ Silk brocade end-panels from an early (possibly Song, 960–1279) mounting of the *Admonitions* scroll. The ink orchid was painted by the Qianlong emperor. The *Admonitions* painting was formerly mounted where there is now a section of plain mounting silk, to the right, as suggested by the half bridging seals to each side.

68 ■ Attributed to Li Gonglin (*c.* 1049–1106). *Shu River.* Detail of a handscroll; ink on paper, 32.2 × 746.5 cm. Freer Gallery, Smithsonian Institution, Wahington DC.

long hours of study to the improvement of his skills as a Confucian ruler, he was also a many-sided actor who created images of himself as an ideal ruler for each racial and religious group within the vast Qing empire. He was quite able to define the meaning of a symbol such as the orchid to suit his agenda. His use of the orchid symbol, for instance, prevented other possible readings, which may have reflected badly on him, from surfacing. For example, the orchid could also be a symbol of the talented minister whose loyalty is spurned by the ruler in favour of sycophants and charlatans. For his part, the Qianlong emperor zealously investigated and 'corrected' all forms of political dissent during his reign.

A major addition to the scroll is a colophon the Qianlong emperor prepared for it at the Pavilion of Tranquil Ease (Jingyixuan) 'five days before midsummer' in the year 1746, at the time of its remounting in the palace works department. This is the last section of the 'colophons panel' (see fig. 73). In this essay written in middle-sized running-script calligraphy, he crows over having just acquired what he considered his four most important paintings: the *Admonitions*, together with three he believed to be by the late Northern Song master Li Gonglin, *Xiao and Xiang Rivers* now in Tokyo National Museum (fig. 65), *Shu River* in the Freer-Sackler collection in Washington DC (fig. 68), and *Nine Songs* now in the Palace Museum, Beijing (fig. 69). (None is today believed to be by Li Gonglin.) Overjoyed at having reunited four scrolls that had been owned by Gu Congyi and praised by Dong Qichang, he celebrated what he called the Reunion of Four Beauties by having all four scrolls housed in his residential quarter, the Pavilion of Tranquil Ease, where they would be at his disposal (fig. 70). To celebrate the Reunion, Qianlong also commanded the scholar-official Dong Bangda (1699–1769) to paint a pair of hanging scrolls entitled *Reunion of Four Beauties* (fig. 71). In them, the emperor is seen in the Pavilion of Tranquil Ease relaxing and looking at a scroll. The building has been transported away from the Forbidden City to the more atmospheric surroundings of a

mountain retreat. The emperor even set aside a corner of this quarter to house and provide space to study these four self-improving works. In so doing, Qianlong restored to
the imperial collection one of the early functions of paintings on furnishings: using
portraits of historical figures to serve as models for the sovereign to avoid or emulate.

Calling the *Admonitions* scroll one of his Four Beauties was a masterly stroke by
which he identified art collecting with enlightened leadership and politics, for the term
Four Beauties also referred to the traditional four accomplishments of the virtuous
ruler, 'ruling, tranquilizing, manifesting, and glorifying'. When we look at the other
three of the Four Beauties, it also becomes clear how he had them outfitted and
mounted as a set. He used the same blue brocade for the outer wrappers, he wrote them
all title-pieces and colophons, and sketched his own paintings on them, and also commanded four scholar-official painters to provide painting-colophons for them. The
Admonitions scroll's painting-colophon, entitled *Pine, Bamboo, Rock and Spring* (fig.
72), was done by a leading flower painter, Zou Yigui (1686–1774). It depicts two pines
and a cypress tree growing among rocks, bamboo and wild orchids by a spring. Visually, the purpose of the painting was to create a frame for the enormous imperial seal
in the centre, which declares that the scroll is one of his imperial majesty's treasures.
The branches of the plants, which themselves are longstanding symbols of virtue and
humanity, reach out affectionately towards the imperial seal, which stands in for the
body of the emperor himself. The Reunion of Four Beauties is recorded in one of the
last entries in the emperor's first catalogue of his imperial painting collection, *Precious
Cabinets of the Stony Gully, First Edition*, which was completed very shortly after the
'Reunion' in 1747.

69 ■ Attributed to Li Gonglin
(*c*.1049–1106). *Illustrations of
the Nine Songs of Qu Yuan.*
Details of a handscroll; ink
on paper, 44.4 × 714 cm.
Palace Museum, Beijing
(on loan from the History
Museum).

70 ■ Dong Hao (1740–1818). *Flowering Plum Trees in the Pavilion of Tranquil Ease*, with inscription by the Qianlong emperor dated 1774. Hanging scroll; ink and colour on paper, 80.6 × 121 cm. National Palace Museum, Taipei.

71 ■ Dong Bangda (1699–1769). *Reunion of Four Beauties*, with inscription by the Qianlong emperor dated 1746. Pair of hanging scrolls; ink on paper, the right, 171.7 × 111.8 cm, the left, 172 × 111.6 cm. National Palace Museum, Taipei.

Including various seals impressed after his painting and inscriptions, the Qianlong emperor stamped in all some several dozen seals on the *Admonitions* scroll and the painting itself in the course of his long reign (1736–95). We know he imposed a cap on the number of imperial seals that could be impressed on paintings, but it is also likely, since he kept the Four Beauties in his private quarters, that he viewed the scroll frequently. In fact, a study of what seals he stamped, where and when would be worthy of another book. One of his seals (the one above Lady Ban) for instance celebrates his being the father of five generations of his family, and another (above the lady in the penultimate scene), his eightieth birthday. It is almost as if he attributed these blessings to his possession of the *Admonitions* scroll.

When the Qianlong emperor acquired the *Admonitions* scroll he wrote that he had received a 'divine omen from antiquity'. In short, for him, possessing this object corroborated his mandate to rule China, as well as the conservative political ideology by which he governed. As far as its authorship went, believing that it was by Gu Kaizhi was enough: he had little interest in Gu's reputation for ribaldry and practical jokes, which were probably 'beyond the pale' in the eyes of this mawkish and sober-minded emperor.

72 ■ Zou Yigui (1686–1774). *Pine, Bamboo, Rock and Spring*, painting-colophon done for the *Admonitions* scroll, *c.* 1746.

The modern theory that the *Admonitions* scroll is not by Gu Kaizhi but a copy made in the Tang dynasty is first seen in writing in a book of 1816 by Hu Jing (1769–1845), *Records of Xijing*, not long after the Qianlong emperor's death. Hu Jing's record is somewhat confusing, however. First of all, he repeats the information given in the Qianlong imperial painting catalogue of 1746–7, including the incorrect statement that the painting is on paper (it is on silk). Perhaps Hu Jing repeated the mistake because he never saw the painting, or it could be a scribe's error. It is also possible that out of respect for the late emperor, who was never contradicted in his lifetime, Hu Jing did not alter details of the written record. During the nineteenth century, there was a related practice among the Manchu imperial family of closing off buildings in the Forbidden City in which past emperors had lived. For them, filial piety was a guiding principle, and showing respect evidently meant changing nothing. There was also a practice among curators in China's museums, set up in the twentieth century, of not changing the attributions of paintings out of respect for the connoisseurship of one's forbears.

If this was the case, why did he then say the painting was a Tang copy? If Hu Jing was showing respect to Qianlong, it is possible that this dating was the emperor's personal unpublished view. Whatever the origin of this theory, it was in tune with the prevailing intellectual mood in the second half of the Qing, the period of the 'evidentiary scholarship' (*kaozheng*) movement. This was characterized by a profound scepticism about the truth of the Chinese past as it had come down written 'on paper'; only history written in stone or metal, as it were, was free from the biases of editors and historians. A Tang date may have satisfied the sceptical outlook of scholars.

In 1899, a rebellion known in the West as the Boxer Rebellion broke out. When the Qing government, then dominated by the Empress Dowager Cixi (1835–1908), lost control of the country and capital, the imperial family left the Forbidden City and went into hiding. Since the Western legations in Beijing were besieged by Boxers, allied troops were dispatched to China from different parts of the globe to quell the rebellion. In the summer of 1900, the Western world anxiously followed the lifting of the siege and crushing of the rebels. The British had sent Indian Army troops from India, including units of the Bengal Lancers. This was the regiment of Capt. Clarence A. K. Johnson (1870–1937), the man who now acquired the *Admonitions* scroll in the capital region in the aftermath of the rebellion, while stationed at the Summer Palace, the imperial family's retreat some ten miles north-west of the city. According to Johnson's descendants, he provided safe passage to a 'lady of high birth' and her family who were in distress, in return for which he was given the scroll.

Johnson's story cannot be proved or disproved, but we can confirm that the *Admonitions* and the other three of the Four Beauties had been transferred to the Summer Palace: a late nineteenth-century palace record notes an order from the Empress Dowager to move them there because the building they had been housed in was to undergo repairs. When Johnson travelled to London in 1902, he took the scroll to the British Museum, it is said, to have its jade toggle evaluated. The then keepers of the sub-department of Oriental Prints and Drawings, the poet Laurence Binyon (1869–1943) and his boss Sir Sidney Colvin (1845–1927), recognized the painting as something special, and arranged for the museum to buy it for the relatively modest sum of £25. It received its acquisition number in the following spring, along with two sixteenth-century books (bought for £20.17s.0d) and two mezzotint portraits of George IV (r. 1820–30) and Lord Lovat (bought for £27.0s.0d), and various less expensive items. Binyon and Colvin set about researching the painting at once.

In the first decade of the twentieth century, Qing delegations toured Europe presenting Chinese art treasures and gifts as reparations for allied lives lost in the Boxer Rebellion. Although the *Admonitions* did not reach London by this means, its acquisition by the British Museum may have been seen in a similar light. In their appraisal of the scroll for the Trustees of the British Museum, Binyon and Colvin consulted a number of experts in the field of Chinese painting. These included a Mr Kohitsu, then considered 'the chief expert of Japan'; Arthur Morison, whose collection of Chinese paintings entered the museum about this time; and two Sinologists, Herbert Giles (1845–1935) and Edouard Chavannes (1865–1918). In about 1910, the doyen of the European Renaissance painting world, Bernard Berenson (1865–1959), who collected early Chinese painting, was supplied with a set of photographs. Later, eminent scholars such as the French explorer Paul Pelliot (1878–1945) lectured on it.

By about 1910, news of its arrival in London had spread across the world, and international scholars were calling upon the museum to publish the scroll. Doubting the ability of Oxford University Press to do the job well using photographic technology, Colvin commissioned a team of visiting Japanese print-makers and a scroll-mounter to produce a hundred woodblock-printed replicas, which went on sale in 1912

73 ■ The *Admonitions* today. Above: colophons panel. Below: paintings panel. The arrow marks the position of the painting in the Qianlong emperor's scroll mounting of *c.* 1746.

for more than £7. Taki Seiichi (1873–1945), editor of Japan's leading art historical journal, *Kokka*, agreed to review the 1912 replica. Binyon took one with him on a lecture tour of the United States shortly before the First World War.

In 1910, the *Admonitions* had its first major exhibition in Britain, in which it was accompanied by Buddhist paintings that had been recently brought back from Dunhuang in the far west of China by the explorer and scholar Sir Marc Aurel Stein (1862–1942). In 1914, the new North Wing of the museum was inaugurated in honour of King Edward VII (r. 1901–10), and it is there that the scroll has since been housed.

World War I to the present

Most of the *Admonitions* scroll is today mounted on two long stretchers, the Western-style format into which it was transformed from a Chinese handscroll in the period of the First World War for reasons of conservation. One holds the extant nine scenes of the painting itself, which measures 25.0 high by 348.5 cm long (fig. 73). The other holds most of the remaining contents of the *Admonitions*' previous life as a handscroll (colophons, end-panels, and so on; 25.0 × 329.0 cm). The Qianlong brocade protective wrapper and Zou Yigui's colophon-painting from the former scroll were not mounted

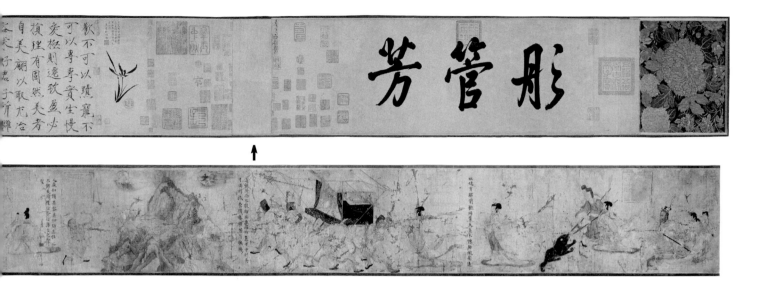

on this stretcher, as they would presumably have made it too long for practical purposes. Also without a place in the new mounting was the jade toggle used to fasten the former scroll, but now redundant.

The purpose of dismantling the scroll was to conserve better what was initially believed to be a genuine work by Gu Kaizhi, to prevent further stress being caused to the artwork by repeated rolling and unrolling. This is an issue that continues to face many museums today; some of these institutions now employ a modern Japanese technique of remounting scrolls on to large rollers designed to reduce stress on the media. One imagines it was also more satisfying to the early twentieth-century Western eye to see the painting as a free-standing picture, and not within the confines of all the Chinese writing. Intriguingly, however, in freeing the scroll of one set of historical conditions, this reconstruction of it could not but impose a set of new ones. The need to conserve a picture for posterity, and, importantly, to make it accessible to viewers were then and remain today worthy goals of the late-modern museum.

For the purpose of making a detailed map of the repairs and damage, the Japanese art historian Fukui Rikichirō was granted a lengthy period of access to the *Admonitions* following its remounting. (Recently, this process has been made more scientific with the use of infrared and ultraviolet photography.) Fukui was part of a Japanese art

74 ■ Maeda Seison (1885–1977). 'Lady Ban declines to ride in the imperial palanquin', copy on paper of the Lady Ban scene in the London *Admonitions* scroll, 1923. Tohoku University, Sendai, Japan.

delegation that toured Europe and the Mediterranean in 1922–3. His delegation also included two leading painters of the Nihonga – literally, 'Japanese painting' – school, Maeda Seison (1885–1977) and Kobayashi Kokei. At this time, Nihonga was undergoing modernization as Japanese painters learned to blend Western realist techniques with East Asian linear expression. While staying in London between March and June 1923, Seison and Kokei were engaged by Fukui to make a precise copy of the *Admonitions* in the British Museum. They accomplished the task in a little less than two months under what Seison later described as uncomfortable conditions, putting in long hours of meticulous work in a dark, smoky atmosphere. Kokei completed the middle three scenes, the 'toilette' (fig. 36), 'bedroom' and 'family' scenes, while Seison copied the first and last three scenes, 'Lady Feng', 'Lady Ban' (fig. 74), and the mountain and hunter, as well as the 'rejection', 'meditation' and the instructress. This trip was a major turning point in their careers, for they returned to Japan not only embracing Western classicism (*yōga*, or 'foreign painting' techniques), but also, through their work on the

Admonitions, having rediscovered some of the basics of East Asian painting: modulation of line, harmony of colour wash, and concern with presenting the immanence of a subject. Kokei's *Hair* of 1931 (fig. 35) came directly out of his copy of the 'toilette' scene in the *Admonitions*. This important Nihonga painting was even turned into a postage stamp in 1969. Seison also followed up his study with linear portrayals of women like *Women Bathing* of 1956.

Professor Fukui returned to Tohoku University in Sendai, Japan, where he taught, with the *Admonitions* copy and a set of photographs, and arranged an exhibition in 1925. He sent an illustrated brochure of the exhibition to friends he had made in London, including the collector George Eumorfopoulos (1863–1939). The copy of the *Admonitions* scroll remains in the collection of Sendai University today, where it is occasionally exhibited. The tradition of making close copies of masterworks stretches back to the beginning of Chinese art history. Indeed, the 'making of copies' was a valuable learning exercise for the painter as well as a means to record and disseminate images, and appeared as number six in the canonical Six Laws of Painting written down by Xie He. As we will find in the next chapter, Chinese artists today continue to learn from the *Admonitions* by making close copies of it.

Technology has played a significant role in how reproductions of the *Admonitions* have been created over the centuries. We have noted that the Beijing copy could have been made as a record of the original by a Southern Song court painter and scribe in the late twelfth century. By the late Ming dynasty, advances in woodblock print technology made mechanical reproductions of this type widely available. Dong Qichang, for instance, reproduced the calligraphic inscriptions on the painting this way. It is fascinating that Sidney Colvin still preferred the Eastern medium of the woodblock print over Western photographic reproduction when he commissioned the replica of 1912. Professor Fukui was fortunate enough to take both, the 1922 painted copy and photographs, back to Japan with him. By the 1920s and '30s, the *Admonitions* was widely published in books, and could now be studied by anyone.

The next time that the British Museum sought to publish the entire scroll was in 1966, under the direction of the then Keeper, Basil Gray (1904–89). Gray collaborated with a team of Japanese photographers from the Kyoto publishing house Benridō, to produce a boxed collotype replica in the form of a handscroll. What is interesting is that it recreated an imaginary *Admonitions* scroll, in a form predating its

Qianlong remounting of *c.* 1746. In 1912, the *Admonitions* was still in this Qianlong mounting, and the 1912 replica had featured that emperor's blue brocade outer wrapper. In 1966, the *Admonitions* was mounted on two long stretchers. The 1966 replica reverted to using the Song dynasty *kesi* tapestry (fig. 54) for the wrapper, and inside, reproduced the Song dynasty brocade end-panels at either end of the painting. No doubt it was more attractive to think of the scroll in its Song mounting than in its Qianlong one. In his accompanying essay, Gray reviewed many decades of controversy over the dating and authorship. He himself argued, mainly on the basis of the calligraphic style of the inscriptions, that the painting was probably a copy of a Gu Kaizhi made in the early Tang dynasty.

Until the last twenty years, it was largely European, Japanese and American scholars and Japanese painters and craftsmen who studied the *Admonitions* at first hand. Remarkably, it has not yet become clear which, if any, Chinese scholars or painters visited the *Admonitions* in the decades after its arrival in London. Between the founding of the Republic of China and the Japanese annexation of north and east China in the 1930s, many painters did travel from China to Europe and were attached to conservatories, mainly in Paris and Berlin, but their primary concern was in learning first-hand about Western realism. Painters interested in traditional brush painting were less likely to have travelled abroad to train or research paintings, although some travelled to Japan, where Western realism had become part of the new language of Japanese ink painting.

The first major exhibition of the *Admonitions* was in 1910, as noted, when it was still a scroll, but in 1990, it was considered too valuable to accompany the pick of the British Museum collection to an exhibition, 'The Brush Dances and the Ink Sings', at the Hayward Gallery in London's South Bank centre of the arts. Although in the 1970s and '80s, it had been on permanent view (illuminated by push-button timed lighting), now, for conservation reasons, it is kept behind a screen in storage. In 2001, when an international colloquy on the *Admonitions* scroll was held at the British Museum, it was the centrepiece of the accompanying exhibition 'Emperors and Court Ladies: Chinese Figure Painting' (fig. 75).

At the turn of the twenty-first century, advances in computer technology and digital imaging have made information and images accessible from almost anywhere on the globe. One can view a 'virtual' copy of the *Admonitions* online at the British

Museum's 'Compass' website, for instance. This technology is so new that we are still only beginning to understand the possibilities it could hold for the future study of art and artefacts, although it is hard to imagine there could be any substitute for the experience of study at first hand.

75 ■ 'Emperors and Court Ladies: Chinese Figure Painting'. Exhibition at the British Museum, June–August 2001. Photo: Glenn Ratcliffe.

5 | Epilogue

The *Admonitions* scroll came to world attention in the first decade of the twentieth century, at the tail-end of an era of profound intellectual scepticism in China about the truth of the past as conveyed in books. Painters, like scholars at this time, were deeply concerned with epigraphic inscriptions in ancient metal and stone objects, which unlike books and manuscripts were by their nature free from the prejudices and biases of editors and copyists over the intervening centuries. Artists developed styles inspired by studies of calligraphic inscriptions on ancient bronze vessels and stone (stele and cliffs, for instance). After the fall of the Manchu Qing dynasty and the foundation of a native Republic of China in 1912, Western realism, with its links to science, reason and 'progress', was posited as a basis for Chinese modernization.

Critics have remarked upon the irony of the Eastern embrace of realism at this time, just as artists in the West were travelling in the opposite direction, towards expressionism, long an ideal in East Asian art. Nonetheless, pictorial realism would trigger a revival in figure painting in twentieth-century China – and in Japan. In the discussion of the *Admonitions* scenes above, we remarked upon the meticulous copies made by two leading Japanese Nihonga painters, Maeda Seison and Kobayashi Kokei, during their European tour of 1922–3. In making these studies, they were investigating the roots of a common East Asian painting tradition, urged on perhaps by a notion of pan-Asian solidarity, which Japan was promoting at this time. Their experiences in copying the London *Admonitions* surfaced again and again as the lineament, colour and subject matter of their subsequent work developed.

China's transition to modernity over the last century differed from Japan's, as did the engagement with the *Admonitions* of those countries' painters. The pioneering Chinese modernizer Xu Beihong (1895–1953), who trained in Paris after the First World War, visited the British Museum in 1919, and later praised the realism in the

Elgin marbles in his writings. However, his silence about one of the great early works of Chinese realism, the *Admonitions*, is worth pointing out. If he saw it, perhaps he did not care to mention it. His own painting indicates little overt interest in it: his early figure studies of the 1920s, and the allegories of national revival of the late 1920s, the '30s and '40s are conservative realist works. The figures in Xu Beihong's paintings were often based on life drawings done in places he lived, visited and exhibited, including France, Singapore and India, rather than referring to figures in old master paintings. The small number of works by Xu Beihong that refer to the art of Gu Kaizhi are almost footnotes to his major interest, described above. One early sketch by Xu shows a painter 'dotting the eye' to bring a painted dragon to life (fig. 76) — the skill for which Gu Kaizhi was celebrated in Shangguan Zhou's woodblock portrait and modern picture-book illustration (see fig. 5). Another is a line painting of one of the ladies of the Xiang, a subject closely linked to Gu Kaizhi in history, in which Xu Beihong tried to marry his Western training in life drawing with Chinese ink-outline drapery style (fig. 77).

76 ■ Xu Beihong (1895–1953). *Painting a Dragon, Dotting the Eye*, 1922. Charcoal, 61 × 44.5 cm. Xu Beihong Museum, Beijing.

Another case is that of the traditional ink-painter Liu Haisu (1896–1994), who was in Europe in the late 1920s and again in 1933–5 to organize exhibitions. He did mention the *Admonitions* painting in a 1935 essay entitled 'Garden of National Painting' (Guohua yuan), but only to say that the *Admonitions* scroll in the British Museum was removed from China in 1900, and what a pity that was. He had apparently never seen the actual painting, but like other Chinese painters had no doubt studied it in the reproductions printed in books that were by then widely available across the world.

The case of a third important modern Chinese artist, the traditionalist painter Zhang Daqian (1899–1983), is similar. He claimed in his writings to have learned from Gu Kaizhi — referring probably to Gu's linear technique. He had the opportunity to

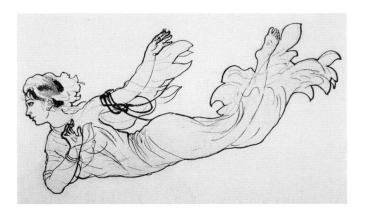

77 ■ Xu Beihong (1895–1953). 'Lady of the Xiang' from the *Nine Songs*, 1942. Detail, ink on paper, 47.5 × 63 cm. Xu Beihong Museum, Beijing.

visit the *Admonitions* as he left China before the Communist take-over in 1949 and was able to travel widely thereafter. Records may yet show that he saw it. Zhang Daqian devoted great effort to copying old masters in his artistic practice (often fooling collectors with the results). He exhibited in the 1960s in London, and, as is well known, sold the British Museum one of his forgeries of the tenth-century master, Juran. His paintings document an interest in the female figure that moved away from the figural types in the *Admonitions*, however.

Zhang had learned to paint figures from medieval Buddhist cave murals at Dunhuang in northwest China during World War II, and at the Ajanta caves in India after it. For him, a beauty was not necessarily a demure Chinese woman. She could be an Indian, Japanese, Nepalese, Central Asian or Brazilian – more of a reflection of his on-going search for a home outside his homeland.

With Fu Baoshi (1904–65) we come to a painter who did study both the line and the female imagery of the *Admonitions* – through photographic reproductions. Fu also studied painting in Japan between 1932 and 1935, learning how Japanese Nihonga painters were incorporating Western realist techniques such as shading and modelling, which gave figures volume in space, to create a properly modern East Asian style. Fu also helped to translate his teacher Kinbara Seigo's (1888–1963) illustrated *History of Chinese Painting* (1935) into Chinese, and is today seen in Japan as a great figure in Chinese-Japanese artistic exchange. But in 1943 in the Chinese wartime capital Chongqing in southwest China, Fu turned his learning and skill against Japan's imperialist forces, then occupying most of China, as well as against the Chinese nationalist government that was unable to expel them. This was in a 1943 painting entitled *Lady of the Xiang* (fig. 78), now in the collection of the Chinese Communist Party leadership, on which Fu noted that he used the *Admonitions* scroll by Gu Kaizhi as a source for the figure.

In modern China, the whole issue of a person's loyalty to his or her ruler or leader continues to be approached in the visual arts via stories of female exemplars, such as the two ladies of the Xiang – the two beautiful daughters that the sage-king

Yao gave to his worthy successor Shun. According to legend, after learning of his death, the ladies drowned themselves in the Xiang River rather than devote themselves to another, and so came to symbolize a person's undying loyalty to a just and worthy cause. These figures, either together or singly, were the basis for many more paintings of this image, illustrating Fu Baoshi's lament at the failure of a great leader to realize national unity. Even after the Chinese civil war, as late as the 1950s, Fu Baoshi was still painting this lyrical theme. The figures in his *The Two Ladies of the River Xiang* (fig. 79), for instance, recall the last two ladies from the London *Admonitions* scroll (fig. 80), which points again to Fu's association of this subject with Gu Kaizhi.

The communist victory in the civil war in 1949 ushered in half a century of national modernization projects and political campaigns in China. In the late 1950s, smarting from the outpouring of criticism of the party and state generated by the Hundred Flowers Movement (1956–7), the authorities staged a revolutionary backlash – the Great Leap Forward (1958–60) – and many artists were labelled rightists. For intellectuals, an important component of this movement, which was geared to propel the nation into modernity, was the Great Leap Forward in education. Between about 1958 and 1962, when the art academies closed and artists were sent to the country so as to learn from the people, a flurry of new studies on Gu Kaizhi appeared in China by leading painters and art scholars. Individuals including Fu Baoshi, as well as Yu Jianhua (1895–1979) and Pan Tianshou (1897–1971), were now collectively drawn to study Gu Kaizhi's art with the aim of trying to define the revolutionary function of the artist in Chinese socialism. However, the Japanese art-historian Kohara Hironobu, writing at the outset of the 'Great Proletarian Cultural Revolution' in China (1966–76), believed that not one of these studies had provided any 'ground-breaking' ideas about the artist and his oeuvre.

In illustrated texts on painting in 1954 and again in 1958, Fu Baoshi, like others, had adopted a Chinese revolutionary tone. He described the art historians of 'capitalist countries', who had been so excited by having the *Admonitions* scroll in London, as 'so-called scholars and specialists', and charged the British Museum with having severed the colophons from the painting to 'launder' the object and make it a British national treasure. The 1958 study by the traditional artist and critic, Pan Tianshou, aimed to relate Gu's style to contemporary 'socialist realism', the official style imported from China's communist neighbour, the Soviet Union:

78 ■ Fu Baoshi (1904–65). *Lady of the Xiang*, dated 1943. Hanging scroll; ink and colour on tan paper, 121 × 35.3 cm. Zhongnanhai Collection.

79 ■ Fu Baoshi (1904–65). *The Two Ladies of the River Xiang, c.* 1950s. Hanging scroll (?); ink and colour on paper, 112.6 × 72.9 cm. Nanjing Museum.

One may say that no painter from the Jin [dynasty, 317–419] to the present has been able to make a single step beyond his scope. Gu Kaizhi's ideology of painting, laid out in the adjacent chart [see fig. 81], is in total accord with the creative principles of today's socialist realism. He is, therefore, the great painting master of our country, having lived in an age of realism fifteen hundred years before our time. He shines like the brightest, most incandescent star in the darkness upon our country's painting world, and brings forth from us of a later age our most heartfelt respect and praise.

Writing of the *Admonitions* itself, Pan also adopted the anti-imperialist rhetoric of the day. After noting Capt. Johnson's 1900 acquisition of the scroll, he remarked that the painting was

> … now in the collection of the British Museum in London, England, with the consequence that painters in our country who would study Gu Kaizhi are unable to see the original and can only do so from reproductions. This is indeed a great shame.

Intriguing is Pan's assumption, common in artistic practice, that the *Admonitions* is a work by Gu Kaizhi and that it is a masterpiece of Chinese line painting.

The political conditions between the mid-1950s and late 1970s, however, cannot have been conducive to the study of figure painting. From the time of the anti-rightist movement and Great Leap Forward in late 1950s, Fu Baoshi and other leading figure painters including Wu Guanzhong (b. 1919), who had trained in Paris from 1947–50, abandoned the figure for landscape. By the second year of the Cultural Revolution, Wu Guanzhong had felt compelled to burn all his oil paintings of the nude as a precaution against political persecution. None survives. Taught to paint in Chinese media by Pan Tianshou, Wu Guanzhong was able to reinvent himself as a pure landscapist. He has never returned to figure painting, even after the beginning of the political thaw in the early 1980s. When Wu had his first solo exhibition in the United States in 1988, he explained to his viewers: 'I spent half my life painting nudes, but for social and historical reasons, I had to abandon painting the human figure and concentrate instead on landscape.' Landscape was, politically, a safer genre.

Another figure painter who abandoned the figure was Lin Fengmian (1900–91), who had trained in the conservative style from 1919–26 in Paris. Lin chose to remain

80 ■ Two palace ladies from the scene of the instructress in the London *Admonitions* scroll. The British Museum.

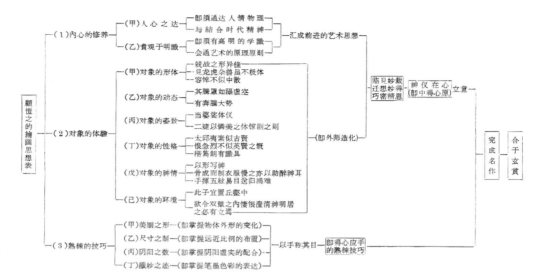

81 ■ Pan Tianshou (1897–1971). 'Diagram of Gu Kaizhi's Ideology of Painting', from Pan Tianshou, *Gu Kaizhi* (1958).

in China with his French wife after 1949, and painted some Chinese-Fauvist odalisque paintings into the 1960s, but like many artists he was jailed in the Cultural Revolution. Released and given official leave in the late 1970s to visit Hong Kong, he chose not to return to China and remained in the colony until his death in 1991. Only there, in that 'window on China', did Lin Fengmian return to painting the nude, working always within the parameters of Chinese line and colouring, within the Chinese figural tradition marked out in the *Admonitions*.

Back in 1958, a time when paintings and painters were judged by their political faults or merits within the communist revolution, Pan Tianshou's linking of Gu Kaizhi's realism with the 'principles of today's socialist realism' marks a brave attempt to play down the *Admonitions*' subject – a 'feudal' criticism of the ruler's wife's conduct – while salvaging its artistic transformations for posterity.

Intriguingly, Pan's diagram of Gu Kaizhi's 'ideology of painting' (fig. 81) corresponds to the crafted structural design of his own paintings, which are noted for their movement and counter-movement, rhythm, momentum, eddies and currents, and ink tonalities. Pan Tianshou's *Various Subjects* (fig. 82), dated 1959, illustrates this nicely. The fluid arrangement of forms along this scroll, rising and falling forms interspersed by formal lulls and eddies, creates a momentum that carries the eye in the traditional

right-to-left direction in a handscroll painting. Pan's Gu Kaizhi diagram is similarly plotted, although because book printing in China had just changed to the Western format, it reads from left to right. The diagram sketches the route Pan discerns between Gu Kaizhi's 'ideology of painting' at the left, through (1) his self-cultivation, (2) his objective experience, and (3) his consummate technique, to the 'profound appreciation' of his artistic achievement at the right.

Pan Tianshou maintained a traditional belief in the inherent goodness of humanity. His painting indicates how ideas of human beauty and integrity could be displaced from bodies to ancient symbols such as bamboo, rocks and orchids, which exemplify human ideals by virtue of their habitat and growth pattern, material form, bearing, lifespan, and immanent character. In the mould of the composer of the 'Admonitions' essay, Zhang Hua, Pan believed that art should be an expression of the artist's moral stature, something Pan himself was able to realize though this calligraphic self-expression; the moral self-cultivation of the individual, expressed this way, could contribute to the development of a just, humane society and government.

One of Pan's *Various Subjects* is the orchid in the wild, which, it will be recalled, was the same subject the Qianlong emperor selected to paint on to one of the end-panels of the *Admonitions* scroll. The emperor's inscription celebrated the orchid's 'beauty in chaste retirement'. Pan's orchid is accompanied by the following inscription in cursive script:

> As alluring as wisps of hair on the retiring Lady Wen's temples,
> As pure as the frozen snow, surpassing the fairy lady,
> Its character may be compared to that of a sage-king;
> It is not only [the orchid's] gentle fragrance that will endure.

82 ■ Pan Tianshou (1897–1971). *Various Subjects*, dated 1959. Detail of a handscroll; ink on paper, 22.2 × 274.6 cm. Metropolitan Museum of Art, New York (Gift of Robert Hatfield Ellsworth, in memory of La Ferne Hatfield Ellsworth, 1986) 1986.267.315.

Calling to mind both ancient and modern readings of the orchid as a symbol of human beauty, purity and morality, Pan insists that it is not just its 'gentle fragrance' that would outlast the present, but also what it stands for. The first line compares the orchid's long leaves to wisps of hair on a retiring beauty's head; it suggests how the allure of the orchid is as irresistible as the attraction of a beautiful woman. The second line compares the white colour of the orchid's flower to snow to point out the flower's unblemished character. In the third line, its character is likened to that of a sage-king. Could this have been a veiled admonition to the 'great helmsman' of the day, Chairman Mao, we wonder, to recall the standards of modesty and integrity by which both the ruler and the artist are judged? The human values evoked in the poem have their counterpart in the visual interest created by the calligraphic movement and structure in the painting.

At this time, the late 1950s, the private art market was abolished by the state, and all art in the PRC was becoming overtly revolutionary. The year 1958, for instance, saw the completion of China's most important political monument, Memorial Stele of the People's Heroes in Tian'anmen Square in Beijing, carved with an inscription in Mao's calligraphy. The following year, 1959, saw a major national exhibition titled after a line of Mao's landscape poetry. Paintings in exhibitions of this period, especially those glorifying Mao's leadership, became strikingly large. One such, Shi Lu's (1919–82) *Fighting in Northern Shaanxi* of 1959, which depicts Mao standing on a mountain top gazing at the distant conflict, measures 238×216 cm, and was mounted on a massive wooden frame. By contrast, Pan Tianshou's traditional handscroll depicting the 'gentle fragrance' of the wild orchid is deliberately but subtly out of kilter.

Pan Tianshou's traditional moral stance in his painting, and his attempt to make the past critically relevant to the revolution made him a target during the Cultural Revolution. In 1966 when the subject of one of his works (an eagle) was misinterpreted he was banned from painting, and then in the early 1970s Red Guards incited by Mao Zedong's wife Jiang Qing (1914–91) hounded Pan to death for being a traditionalist. Like Zhang Hua, Pan was driven by loyalty and duty, and like the *Admonitions*, his work comes across as a tribute to the integrity of the human mind.

After Mao's death and the arrest of the 'Gang of Four' led by Jiang Qing in 1976, a phase of tentative modernization and opening up to the outside world began. In the late 1970s the art academies began to reopen. At the Central Academy of Fine

Arts in Beijing, enlarged old reproductions of the *Admonitions*, which had perhaps even survived from the 1920s or '30s, were brought out for students on the foundation painting course to learn basic line drawing (*baimiao*) by making meticulous copies of the scenes. But by the 1980s some artists found that learning more about traditional Chinese artistic expression meant their moving to the West, where old masterworks by the great names of Chinese painting became accessible to them for the first time.

In the two decades since the open-door policies were initiated, China has undergone further party political campaigns, first against 'spiritual pollution' in the 1980s, and then, tragically, against democracy in 1989. In the 1990s, the 'cynical realist' painters ridiculed an official campaign to promote humanism by using crass images to portray China's 'yob' culture. Other artists continued to leave China for Europe and America, and are today able to travel back and forth, and show their work at international exhibitions and art events. Although it is the avant-garde experimentalism that often grabs the headlines due to official censorship and public outrage, as far as content goes, the human figure and the body remain broadly significant themes in contemporary Chinese art.

Studies of the *Admonitions* today follow different paths in the discovery of new knowledge. One, at least, involves identifying unknown facts about it. There is little likelihood of any fresh evidence coming to light in early written sources; Mi Fu's attribution of the *Admonitions* to Gu Kaizhi remains the authoritative link. Potential new light is thrown on Gu Kaizhi and this scroll, however, each time a related mural is discovered in a tomb. These sources hold much promise for the future as China looks set to enjoy and reflect upon its current 'golden age of archaeology' for many decades to come.

Another important path is tracing the *Admonitions* scroll in the conversations we have about art between cultures. As we begin to think historically about recent Western engagement with Chinese art, it is clear the old monolithic concept of China no longer rings true. In twentieth-century Britain, the examples of the designer and potter Bernard Leach (1887–1979) and the collector and connoisseur Sir Percival David (1892–1964) offer two distinct visions of what Chinese art could be about. For David, it was classical restraint, which he identified in paintings and imperial ceramics, a taste modelled on that of the Qianlong emperor. For Leach, who studied Chinese ceramics in pre-War Japan, it was popular, craft-based exuberance and spirited design.

Reflecting on modern Chinese art, Wen C. Fong has recently written that the 'convergence of the artistic traditions of East and West is the displacement of the mimetic by the expressive', suggesting that representation of the phenomenal world is yielding to a more self-conscious mode of artistic practice. The idea is indeed borne out by the work of the French realist painter Balthus (1908–2001), whose marriage to the Japanese artist Setsuko Ideta in 1967 intensified an exploration of East Asian genre, linearity and colour ongoing since his childhood. Balthus's paired studies of two Japanese women regarding themselves in mirrors, painted between 1967 and 1976 (fig. 83), make an intriguing juxtaposition with the admonition to cultivate inner beauty in the 'toilette' scene from the *Admonitions* scroll. The toilette was an East Asian theme that Balthus employed throughout his painting career, but he probably learned about it at some remove from the *Admonitions* – perhaps via Japanese woodblock prints, or Nihonga. Balthus believed in what he called a 'community of perception' between East

83 ▪ Balthus (Balthasar
Klossowski de Rola;
1908–2001).
Right: *Japonaise à la table
rose (Japanese Woman with
Red Table)*, 1967–76. Oil on
canvas, 145 × 192 cm. Private
collection. Left: *Japonaise au
miroir noir (Japanese Woman
with Black Mirror)*, 1967–76.
Oil on canvas, 150 × 196 cm.
Private collection.

and West that was only interrupted in the (European) Renaissance 'when perspective introduced a more "realistic" conception of representation'. He said that 'the Chinese conception of painting ... aims not at the representation of things, but at an *identification*. The great Western painting is that which does not "know" this rupture with the Oriental.'

Intriguingly, the work of some Chinese artists today is concerned precisely with this question of cross-cultural understanding – or, in the word of one of them, Gu Wenda (b. 1955), 'misunderstanding'. Together with Xu Bing's (see below), Gu Wenda's experimentation with calligraphy in the multi-cultural environment has been profoundly challenging to Chinese tradition, in part because in it calligraphy becomes more of a gateway to than a defensive barrier for Chinese culture. Rebellion here seems to have been triggered by a sense of alienation from one's own culture brought about by political repression and isolation. Gu Wenda's *Babble of the Millennium:*

84 ■ Wenda Gu (b. 1955). *The Babble of the Millennium: United Nations* series, 1999. A tower of pseudo Chinese, English, Hindi and Arabic, and synthesized Chinese-English, made from human hair. H. 2250 cm, d. 1020 cm. Site-specific installation for the San Francisco Museum of Modern Art. Collection of the San Fransisco Museum of Modern Art.

United Nations series (1999), for instance, includes calligraphy in pseudo languages (Chinese, English, Hindi, Arabic and synthesized Chinese-English) made from human hair (fig. 84). In this work, 'scrolls' of calligraphy over 22 metres high hang down to create a Tower of Babel: Chinese calligraphy becomes as much 'non-sense' as any other writing, and yet, paradoxically, supplies the artistic means for conveying the difficulty of cross-cultural understanding.

Xu Bing (b. 1955) is another artist who has invented new calligraphy. His *'The Scholars' by William Butler Yeats* (1998; fig. 85) is a transcription in synthesized Chinese-English writing of verses by the great Irish poet. 'Traditional' Chinese would be read from top to bottom and right to left, whereas western languages are read from left to right, top to bottom. *The Scholars* is a cross between the two, read from top to bottom, left to right. Each word is a 'character' that has been reformulated by the artist into a square by changing the letters of the Roman alphabet into equivalent Chinese calligraphic forms. The letter B thus becomes the Chinese radical element 阝; and A approximates to the form 亼 as in 今, 命 or 合. The first word of the text, 'bald', remotely resembles the Chinese character 險; the third word, 'of', remotely resembles 吁. The letters of each word are combined in the 'character' in the order in which strokes and components would be written, that is, beginning at the top left and working through the square towards the bottom right. By mediating the gap between Chinese and Western cultures, this pseudo-calligraphy thus becomes a blueprint for approaching Chinese calligraphy. It provides an understanding of the role of the text, of handwriting, of the general mechanics

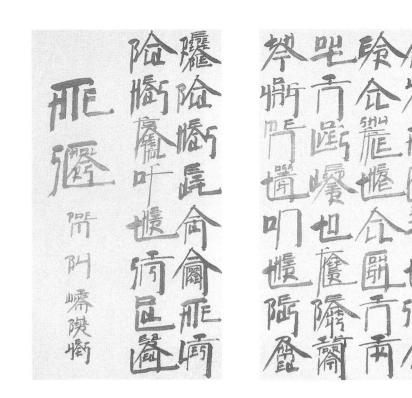

of execution. While it may still appear exotic and strange to the outsider, it is equally so for the so-called insider who knows Chinese calligraphy. This versatility is a great strength of the written language that has helped keep it vibrant and relevant in history.

Chinese and other East Asian artists will necessarily rely on modes and idioms of self-expression from within their own visual cultures because that is what they know. As the embodiment of the first law of painting, 'breath resonance – life motion', the *Admonitions* scroll attributed to Gu Kaizhi stands as perhaps the foundational work of a painting tradition that has looked beyond the representation of things, towards identification and expression; it also illustrates painting's intimate links with the poet's voice and calligrapher's brush. What is so remarkable is the *Admonitions* scroll's power, today as in history, to retain – and shape – our interests in these things in such an open-ended way.

85 ■ Xu Bing (b. 1955). *'The Scholars', Poem by William Butler Yeats*, square word calligraphy poetry, 1998. Three panels; ink on paper, each 89 × 48.3 cm.

References and further reading

In the first instance, the reader is referred to Shane McCausland (ed.), *Gu Kaizhi and the Admonitions Scroll* (London: British Museum Press, 2003) (hereafter McCausland (ed.), *Gu Kaizhi*).

Gu Kaizhi's dates are not certain. The earliest proposed birth date is 341 and the latest death date 407.

Chapter 1

For translations of some early works of painting criticism relating to Gu Kaizhi, see W. R. B. Acker's *Some T'ang and Pre-T'ang Texts on Chinese Painting* (Leiden, reprint, 1984). For further discussion of Gu Kaizhi's painting and his place in the early critics' writings, see Wen C. Fong's 'The *Admonitions* Scroll and Chinese Art History' in McCausland (ed.), *Gu Kaizhi* (the translations of Zhang Yanyuan and Zhang Huaiguan are after Fong's). On Gu Kaizhi's interest in painting eyes, see, e.g., Audrey Spiro, 'New light on Gu Kaizhi: Windows of the soul', *Journal of Chinese Religions*, vol. 16 (1988), pp. 1–17. Mi Fu's self-comparison with Gu Kaizhi is discussed by Peter Sturman in his *Mi Fu: Style and the Art of Calligraphy in Northern Song China* (New Haven & London, 1997), p. 88ff, and by Alfreda Murck in McCausland (ed.), *Gu Kaizhi*. On the *Goddess of the Luo River* scrolls and their relation to Gu Kaizhi see Chen Pao-chen's 'The Goddess of the Lo River: a study of early Chinese narrative handscrolls', PhD thesis, Princeton University, 1987. On the inclusion of these scrolls in Gu Kaizhi's oeuvre in pre-modern times, see Yin Ji'nan's essay in McCausland (ed.), *Gu Kaizhi*. A Song date for the *Admonitions* inscriptions was proposed by the Japanese scholar, Taki Seiichi in the early twentieth century (see Arthur Waley, *An Introduction to the Study of Chinese Painting* [London, 1923], chapter 5).

Chapter 2

Studies of the 'Admonitions' text include one by Hsio-yen Shih in 'Poetry Illustration and the Works of Ku K'ai-chih' in *The Translation of Art: Essays on Chinese Painting and Poetry* (*Renditions*, no. 6, ed. James C. Y. Watt; Hong Kong, 1976), pp. 6–29 (especially for the first four admonitions), and another by Basil Gray (1904–89), a

Keeper of Oriental Antiquities at the British Museum, from an essay he wrote to accompany the 1966 colour collotype replica of the scroll produced in association with the Japanese publishing house Benridō. Gray's translations are, in turn, based on those by the sinologue Arthur Waley (1889–1966), who worked at the British Museum in the first half of the twentieth century. Translations of the Confucian classics may be found in James Legge's *The Chinese Classics* (1861 and reprints). Scenes 1–3: on Chinese mythology and early history see F. W. Mote's *Intellectual Foundations of China* (New York, 1989) and 'Fu Xi and Nü Wu in Han mythology and art' by Mark Lewis in *Art and Religion in Pre-modern China* (tr. & ed. Wang Tao and Roderick Whitfield; London, forthcoming in 2003). The early history of illustrations of Liu Xiang's *Biographies of Exemplary Women* is traced in Wu Hung, *The Wu Liang Shrine: the Ideology of Early Chinese Pictorial Art* (Stanford, 1989), and the text is translated in A. R. O'Hara, *The Position of Women in Early China* (Washington DC, 1945). On the Song copy of the *Admonitions* in Beijing see Yu Hui's 'The *Admonitions* – a Song copy' in *Orientations* (June 2001), pp. 41–51, reprinted in McCausland (ed.), *Gu Kaizhi*. Scene 3: for ancient music, see Kenneth DeWoskin's *A Song for One or Two: Music and the Concept of Art in Early China* (Ann Arbor, 1982), especially pp. 92–4. Scenes 4–5: for the identification of Lady Fu and the translations from the *History of the Former Han* (ch. 97b), see Chen Pao-chen's essay in McCausland (ed.), *Gu Kaizhi*. Scene 6: the translation of the passage of the 'Nymph of the Luo River' is by Hsio-yen Shih (see above, 1976). Scene 7: with other early texts on painting, Xie He's *Classification of Painters (Gu huapin lu)* is translated and annotated in William Acker's 1954 *Some T'ang and Pre-T'ang Texts on Chinese Painting*. On mirrors and the pivoting device see Wu Hung's essay in McCausland (ed.), *Gu Kaizhi*. Scene 12: on literacy among the elite in early China see Michael Nylan, 'The Early Aesthetic Values of Writing and Calligraphy', *Oriental Art*, vol. XLVI, no. 5 (2000), pp. 19–29.

Chapter 3

For further discussion of the calligraphy and the comparisons given here, see the essays by Professors Wen C. Fong, Wu Hung and Yang Xin in McCausland (ed.), *Gu Kaizhi*.

Chapter 4

A set of important studies concerned with the provenance of the *Admonitions* and the historical reputation of Gu Kaizhi are those by Wang Yao-t'ing, Yin Ji'nan, Stephen Little (esp. for Dong Qichang), Nixi Cura, Zhang Hongxing and Charles Mason, and the commentaries on them by Cary Y. Liu and Craig Clunas, in the section 'The Treasure of Empires' in McCausland (ed.), *Gu Kaizhi* (London, 2003). See also Charles Mason, 'The British Museum *Admonitions* Scroll: a Cultural Biography', *Orientations* vol. 32, no. 6 (June 2001), pp. 30–4. Capt. Johnson's explanation to his family of how he acquired the scroll was related to me in a personal communication by Jane Portal (email, 5 March 2002), Assistant Keeper at the British Museum, based on information provided by Johnson's nephew Sir Alastair Stewart, Bt., on a visit to the British Museum the previous day. Stewart's information was related to him by his cousin, Johnson's daughter, Mrs Betty Manzano. Laurence Binyon and Sir Sydney Colvin's activities and projects with the scroll are recorded in reports and minutes in the *Admonitions* scroll's file kept in the Department of Asia (formerly Department of Oriental Antiquities) at the British Museum. The author is most grateful to Robert Knox, the Keeper, for making this important information available. Details of the 1910 exhibition may be found in the booklet accompanying the exhibition. The early British Museum publications of the scroll also include Arthur Waley's *Introduction to the Study of Chinese Painting* (see above), especially chapter 5. The catalogue of the 1990 Hayward Gallery exhibition is by Anne Farrer, *The Brush Dances and the Ink Sings* (London, 1990). The *Admonitions* can be viewed online at www.thebritishmuseum.ac.uk/compass; search: 'admonitions'.

Epilogue

For further reading on the modern Chinese artists discussed in the epilogue, see, e.g., Wen C. Fong's *Between Two Cultures* (New York, 2001) and Michael Sullivan's *Art and Artists of Twentieth-Century China* (Berkeley, 1996). On the use of the lady of the Xiang image by Fu Baoshi, see Alfreda Murck's 'Images that Admonish' in *Orientations* vol. 32, no. 6 (June 2001), pp. 52–7. Professor Kohara's views on early PRC scholarship on Gu Kaizhi are found in his *The 'Admonitions of the Instructress to the Court Ladies' Scroll* (1967, revised 1999–2000; tr. & ed. Shane McCausland; London, 2000). The quotes from Pan Tianshou are from his *Gu Kaizhi* (1958), pp. 36–7 and p. 21, respectively. For Wu Guanzhong's solo US exhibition of 1989 see the catalogue edited by Lucy Lim, *Wu Guanzhong: A Contemporary Chinese Painter* (San Francisco, 1989). For a further study of Pan Tianshou's *Various Subjects* see Wen C. Fong, *Between Two Cultures*, pp. 214–18. Wang Jia'nan and Cai Xiaoli, two London-based artists who were in the first intake of the Central Academy of Fine Arts following its reopening in 1978, provided information about the use of the *Admonitions* in teaching there, as well as about their move to London in the late 1980s (conversation with the author, 29 April 2002; Wang Jia'nan's 'Speech at the British Museum', undated manuscript). Wen Fong's discussion of the convergence of Eastern and Western traditions appears in his *Between Two Cultures*, p. 260, n. 19. Balthus' remarks on art were made in an interview with Philippe Dagan ('Monsieur le comte: a visit with Balthus', tr. Erich Eichman; at http://www.newcriterion.com/archive/10/dec91/erich.html).

Picture credits and sources

Frontispiece, 1, 12, 20, 24, 25, 29, 30, 33, 37, 39, 41, 44, 45, 47, 48, 54, 56, 57, 61, 66, 67 72, 73, 80: © Trustees of the British Museum. **2**: after *Shoron* 11, p. 83. **4**: after *Dunhuang shiqu quanji* (Hong Kong, 1999), vol. 7, no. 207. **10**: after *Shudao quanji* (Taipei, 1989), vol. 4, nos 90–1. **14, 18, 59, 70, 71**: National Palace Museum, Taipei, Taiwan, ROC. **18**: after Fong & Watt, *Possessing the Past* (New York, 1996), pl. 98. **22**: after *Zhongguo gudai shuhua tumu*, vol. 21 (Beijing, 2000), p. 90. **23**: after *Zhongguo meishu quanji* (painting series), vol. 10 (Shanghai, 1989), no. 178. **35**: after *Showa no bunka isan* (Tokyo, 1990), vol. 1, no. 47. **38**: after *Zhongguo meishu quanji* (painting series), vol. 19. **50**: after *Zhongguo meishu quanji* (calligraphy and seals series) vol. 2, p. 193, pl. 104. **52, 53**: after *Shudao quanji* (Taipei, 1989) vol. 5, nos 46 & 74, respectively. **58**: Photo: Bruce M. White. © 2002 Trustees of Princeton University. **63, 64**: after Wan-go Weng, *Chen Hongshou: His Life and Art* (Shanghai, 1997), vol. 2, nos 6.3–4 & no. 99, respectively. **65, 68**: after *Bunjinga suihen*, vol. 2 (Tokyo, 1985), nos 64 & 60, respectively. **76, 77**: after *Xu Beihong huaji* (Beijing, 1988), nos 74 & 101. **79**: after *Paintings of Fu Baoshi* (Beijing, 1992), no. 125. **83**: © ADAGP, Paris and DACS, London 2003. **84**: after *Orientations*, vol. 33, no. 3 (March 2002), p. 104. **85**: after Christie's, *Asian Avant-Garde, Oct.12.98* (London, 1998), lot 48.

Every effort has been made to identify the copyright holders and to obtain their permission to reproduce illustrations. Apologies are made for any inadvertent errors or omissions.

Index